HOMEPLACE

JOHN LINGAN

HOMEPLACE

*A Southern Town,
a Country Legend, and the Last Days
of a Mountaintop Honky-Tonk*

Houghton Mifflin Harcourt

Boston   New York

2018

hmhco.com

Library of Congress Cataloging-in-Publication Data is available.
ISBN 978-0-544-93253-1

Portions of this book originally appeared in the
Morning News, *The Baffler*, and BuzzFeed.

Book design by Chrissy Kurpeski

Printed in the United States of America
DOC 10 9 8 7 6 5 4 3 2 1

Contents

———— ✦ ————

For Justyna

MUSIC SEEKS TO CHANGE LIFE;
LIFE GOES ON;
THE MUSIC IS LEFT BEHIND;
THAT IS WHAT IS LEFT TO TALK ABOUT.

— GREIL MARCUS

Preface

In August 1716, lieutenant governor Alexander Spotswood led sixty-three men and seventy-four horses on an exploratory mission across the Rappahannock River valley and into Virginia's Blue Ridge Mountains. So far as any of them could tell, they were walking into unpassable darkness: the dense ocean of trees was daily shrouded in mist and clouds. The Knights of the Golden Horseshoe, as Spotswood's band of German, Scots-Irish, and Native American muscle was later known, hacked through the forest until finally they found the Swift Run Gap, a narrow pass in present-day Stanardsville. From the peak of the Blue Ridge, they had view of a North American Avalon, an endless horizon of wide skies and pastoral splendor that looked, more than anything, like the lush, mountainous English Lake District that was soon to inspire the Romantic poets. The unblemished Shenandoah Valley was a setting that might leave a man "Alive to all things and forgetting all," as Wordsworth felt about the Lakeland. Spotswood had gone looking for a trade route and ended up in paradise.

From that point on, according to one Indian testimony of the time, the white men "came like flocks of birds." Some crossed the mountains and went north on the Valley's Great Wagon Road, where they encountered Pennsylvania Dutch explorers who had come down through the Cumberland Valley. Within years, the Europeans built houses, barns, roads, a route back to the coastal colonies, and infrastructure for grain and livestock farming. In 1738, a little hamlet called Frederick Town was incorporated on a wide, flat expanse up toward the Potomac River, perfectly positioning it as a trading post. The new settlement attracted craftsmen and Quakers, gentry and rabble. By the time its name was changed to Winchester in 1752, the town was a hub—the de facto capitol of what was then still the Wild West.

The border kept moving, of course, but Winchester maintained its odd duality of economic prominence and cultural seclusion. George Washington commanded troops there during the French and Indian War. In the nineteenth century, it was the biggest commercial market in the Shenandoah and the site of multiple pivotal Civil War battles. And starting between the world wars, it became best known as the home base of Harry Flood Byrd, the most influential southern senator for nearly four decades and the leading grower in the world-famous Valley apple industry. Through all this, for more than two centuries, the social order stayed ironclad. The same wealthy families owned everything—jobs, government, and media—and everyone else just hoped to be employed by them.

By the time I first came to Winchester in early 2013, the apple acreage had been largely replaced by corporate land holdings and housing sprawl. The Washington and Civil War stories had been subsumed into local lore and historical tourism draws. In many ways, twenty-first-century Winchester was just an archetypal early-American town: a cozy historic district circumscribed by highways and big-box shopping, increasingly diverse but still politically conservative and a little dull. The kind of place where people knew their neighbors' genealogy and filled prescriptions at a pharmacy whose perfume shelves were misted over with ancient dust. The sole local paper, the *Winchester Star*, remained independently owned by descendants of Harry Flood Byrd.

I had come to learn about Patsy Cline, who was born in Winchester in 1932 and spent most of her life there, suffering the indignities of wealthy men and women who considered her common. I still don't understand what people think they'll find in an artist's home—some experience *beyond* the art, I suppose, a glimpse of the wide, hidden world that great songs always seem like advertisements for—but when I learned that a legend had grown up less than two hours from my house in the D.C. suburbs, I followed the well-worn path. Thousands of aficionados have gone to Winchester ever since the singer died tragically in 1963, and when you arrive and start asking questions, the Patsy people all tell you: You have to go see Jim McCoy. He was an old man who had known Patsy in his youth, and for years he had owned and operated the Troubadour Bar & Lounge, the only twang-and-sawdust roadhouse left in the Virginias. If you want to understand how this place works, everyone said, you need to head up to Jim's compound in the Blue Ridge of West Virginia and see what he's made.

How right they were. First and foremost, this book is about Jim McCoy, a humble Valley lifer who contributed to a momentous, underappreciated era in American music, and a perfect emblem for all the unheralded working people who made that music what it was. From a drafty mountaintop house without electricity, he managed to create a life and a legacy in entertainment, writing and recording dozens of his own songs and many more of other people's. He made it to Nashville's inner sanctum and eventually to the Opry stage. His story is not a rags-to-riches saga, but something more complex and bittersweet. In a time of extraordinary change and upheaval, as interstates sprang up and the orchards turned to housing tracts, he embodied an older tradition, and empowered many of his neighbors whose livelihoods had become threatened by all this so-called progress. Ultimately, as I saw up close, he suffered in the manner of those neighbors as well.

Over the course of countless nights at the Troubadour and with the people who live near it, I came to see that the Winchester region, for all its sleepiness, was actually in the final throes of a full-scale transformation that began more than a half-century earlier. Starting in the 1950s, a new "business progressive" mindset replaced the previous southern focus on agriculture, and Virginia, the upland Shenandoah in particular, went all in. Shenandoah University, a small Methodist school originally located in Dayton, about an hour south, relocated to the east side of town in 1960. In 1965, a length of Interstate 81, which runs from Tennessee to Canada, opened on the city's eastern border. The Apple Blossom Mall arrived in the mid-1980s and chain stores spread around it like a rash. Virginia's sole inland port was built just 12 miles south of Winchester in 1989, so shipping traffic, of all things, now accounts for part of the region's economic pull as well. The current Winchester-Frederick County Manufacturing Directory includes more than a hundred companies, most of which have come to the area since the late twentieth century.

In the 1980s and 1990s, the Winchester region's expansion rivaled that of any other region in the United States. Inside the Winchester limits alone, the population increased 7.4 percent from 1990 to 2000, and 11 percent from 2000 to 2010. U.S. manufacturing employment decreased throughout the same time, but Winchester-Frederick County's spiked. The first industrial parks were built in the 1980s, and they expanded to cover a shudderingly vast swath of land above the city limits along the interstate. There is new money here, more than ever before, but the inequality is arguably no better than it was in Harry Flood Byrd's time. The region still has manufacturing jobs, but that work is less stable and sufficient than it once was. There is heroin, delivered through all those nearby highways, and widespread health struggles, a result of rising health-care costs. There are immigrants, too, mostly from Mexico and points south, trying and often struggling to find that elusive better life. Turns out that this little town of 25,000 is in fact a brutal microcosm for the entire country, a place where the deepest history and most pressing contemporary concerns are in constant collision.

And so secondly, this book is about the never-ending American fight between commerce and culture, fought, in this case, on a battlefield that is both universal and unique. No region in the United States is safe from corporatization or the loss of local identity, but not every region has experienced such a thorough, rapid dismantling of a centuries-old order, with all the excitement and pain that entails. And not everywhere has a figure like Jim McCoy to reflect and ennoble the struggle of a whole class of people as this transition occurs. When Jim opened the Troubadour in 1986, Winchester's transition to tourist-trap respectability was already inexorable. Jim provided a sanctuary for those people who still remembered the era of cigarettes and cowboy hats, and for those of us who only romanticize it. It was always a place for people who prefer low lights and drunken karaoke to strip malls and antique shopping—anyone who still believed that you can have the best time of your life in a backwoods bar in rural America.

That kind of good time is harder to find each year, but I found it, and saw its significance to a region that is in perpetual risk of losing its strange native character. There is no name for the meeting place of Virginia's western hump and West Virginia's eastern panhandle. Whatever you think it is, it's the edge of that: the northernmost point in the South, the westernmost point in the East, not at all urban but nothing like Appalachia. Some of the oldest money in America lives here, and some of the country's oldest historical ghosts, but it is also home to some of the freshest immigrants and the most dirt-poor red-state white folks. This spot doesn't have a name, but it has an energy, and Jim McCoy is the truest expression of it.

So this is his story, but it's also his neighbors' story and the story of his land. Because my years among all three taught me, more than anything, that none of those stories are possible without the others.

PART ONE

OLD DAYS

1

---✶---

The Blue Ridge Country King

SURE, THERE'S A QUICK WAY to the Troubadour Bar & Lounge: starting from Berkeley Springs, West Virginia, population 624, you simply turn onto Route 38/3, Johnson's Mill Road, and head up into the Blue Ridge. Swing along pendulous mountain curves that ease past wide grass fields, up through dense tunnels of pin oak and pine. Take it slow at the one-lane wooden bridge and again at the hairpin turn by the vaunting power-line interchange. Past the cemetery, with its green-tinted graves so old that the names and dates are just half-disappeared scars. Then on through the final hypnotic stretch of forest, still on a roller-coaster incline that demands another inch down on the gas just as you might be compelled to slow up and address your lord.

Again, that's the quick way, only twenty or so minutes of

alert mountain driving. But if you aren't coming from Berkeley Springs—if you're coming from Capon Bridge, Gerrardstown, Hedgesville, Paw Paw, or any of the dozens of other panhandle towns too small for maps—then it's even longer. Then it's all woods, up and down hills with no visible end, past spray-painted houses made of plywood and exposed Tyvek. Look out for smeared snakes and exploded deer, and prepare for shaky trips across metal bridges high above the Potomac's minor branches. Down below, to the boys swimming in T-shirts and waterproof shoes, your car's faraway rumble might as well be distant thunder.

No matter if you take the back roads or the back-of-back roads, eventually the tree line splits and the road delivers you to Highland Ridge, a stretch of sloping, sunny prairie in Morgan County. When I first arrived, it was relatively populous, after more than a decade of steady development to make room for Baltimore and D.C. retirees. To the east, the state long ago shaved a wide and hideous strip down the mountainside to make way for the electrical towers. But to the west, the Blue Ridge peaks still rolled on for ages, unblemished. Above them stretched miles of epic Shenandoah Valley meteorological scenery, whole weather systems forming and dying above the mountains' dark folds. In his mid-eighties, when his family would rest easier if he had a hospital or even a doctor nearby, Jim McCoy still lived on Highland Ridge. This was by choice, by ornery insistence. He still watched the sky like a farmer: constantly, with a mixture of awe and submission. He still grew tomatoes like prior generations of upland West Virginians who lived too remotely for grocery stores. Jim ran the Troubadour and managed its grounds, but this wasn't only his place of business. Back before those power lines were even a dream in some developer's mind, Jim McCoy was born here, and his intention was to end his life where it started. This, as he called it, was his homeplace.

When I pulled into the parking lot and turned off my car, the daytime quiet was overwhelming. It was a Friday in early June, the opening weekend of the outdoor season. A cracking noise echoed softly in the distance—maybe a gunshot, maybe a splitting log. I could hear every minor breath of wind, every gravel pebble crunching under my feet. I heard soft voices as I pushed open the white picket gate, and saw Jim sitting at one of the white plastic picnic tables out back, smoking a Marlboro Red. His much younger brother and niece were sitting on either side of him, elbows on their knees. They were clearly frustrated by a sudden visitor. Jim was approaching eighty-four at the time, and looked a few hard years beyond that. His attenuated, faintly tattooed forearms stretched out from his faded collared work shirt. He flicked his cigarette and the ashes fell past his blue pants and gray Velcroed shoes, lost in the thick grass. He raised his head and I caught my first up-close glimpse of his strained face underneath a dark trucker's hat. From his eyes alone I could tell that his body had betrayed him. He longed to move and couldn't, at least not easily, not painlessly. So instead he smiled, and instantly came to life.

"They want me to quit working," Jim said, rising from his chair and gesturing to his visitors. Knowing they were beaten, brother and niece helped him up. They were only thinking of his health: Jim was due for gall bladder surgery within a fortnight. Standing wobbly, he straightened his hat brim, and scuttled over to greet me while his relatives traded exasperated glances.

"We'll get going," his brother said, and shook my hand without introducing himself. Jim had entertained his share of curious hangers-on up here, and someone with his best interests at heart might think that another out-of-town Patsy completist would only rile the old man. The wooden gate slapped gently behind his relatives, and Jim put a hand around my upper arm as their car passed over the gravel onto Highland Ridge Road and down into the woods.

We walked out from under the trees, past the picnic tables, playground, and covered bar. Jim stopped at the edge of the hill, taking in the wide sky.

"How you like that?" he asked, pointing at the view. I was taken aback, and said so.

"In the morning I come out here and have my coffee while the sun comes up. In the evening I have my Jim Beam and watch it go down." He laughed hard: a deep, decayed growl. Later on, when I read some of the innumerable articles that have been written about the Troubadour in every small-town paper within a five-hour drive, I saw Jim had repeated this same line to every writer who'd ever stood on the property.

At the bottom of the hill, right at the tree line, sat Troubadour Studios, a musty double-wide where regional bands still came to record, as they had since he opened the facility almost thirty years earlier. (He operated various home studios before that, going back to the 1950s.) The trailer sat next to a covered bandstand that hosted weekend festivals between Memorial Day and Labor Day weekends. And right where we were standing, looming above us like a naval cannon, was Jim's most photographed piece of property: a 10-foot-long six-shooter, the cylinder of which contained a smoker big enough for a whole hog. During outdoor season, hickory-scented smoke poured out of the gun barrel all weekend long and Troubadour Park filled with neighbors, old friends, and outsiders who wanted to see the last honky-tonk standing.

Jim held on to me for balance as we shuffled down the hill. When we reached the trailer he led me into his windowless shrine. CDs and press photos lined the walls, images going back a half-century to the era when he led Joltin' Jim and the Melody Playboys. Jim's stage outfit was a custom-made red suit embroidered with white musical notes, topped with a white Stetson; the Playboys, his five-piece band, backed him in matching black Stetsons and bow-tie suits. In the old photos he was forever grinning crookedly underneath a little pomade twist. He looked muscular, farm-raised. His neck was thick, though his eyes looked tired even then. In the 1950s and 1960s, Jim and his men prowled the state highways of Maryland, Pennsylvania, and the Virginias, playing every dank beer hall and Moose Lodge that would hold them. Poetically, unbelievably, they traveled in a disused hearse. Jim earned the honorific "Joltin'" from putting on so many miles, rushing from recording sessions to radio gigs to late-night shows and back to the farm. But he also knew alliteration would help him build his name, as it had for the Kountry Krackers, his friends and recording clients who served as one of Patsy's earliest local bands.

The recording booths in the studio were made of plywood and soundproofed with decaying eggshell foam. The drums, set apart in one corner room, had tiny divots in the heads, and the bell of the ride cymbal was cracked. As if to apologize and make up for the accommodations, a centerfold featuring a teased blonde with pendulous naked breasts had been pinned to the sagging fabric walls. The hallways and other rooms were crammed floor to ceiling with yellowed newspaper clips, pushpin-damaged photos, and junk-shop grails such as a poster-size "Map to Heaven."

Down the narrow hallway, every room was a makeshift museum: binders full of old ads and record deals in four massive file cabinets, old tape reels stacked in crushed boxes in every nook and corridor, including the space on either side of the toilet. If the Troubadour grounds felt endless, as wide as the sky, the studio was its inverse. There was a whole world in there, but it was subterranean, a tunnel made of old mail.

"There's a fella coming by from the Library of Congress," Jim told me as he puttered around the maze. "Wants to gather some of this stuff up and decide what to keep. I told him good luck. John set that up," meaning local newspaper editor John Douglas, who published a slim, tabloid-size biography, *Joltin' Jim: Jim McCoy's Life in Country Music*, in 2007, right after the old man was inducted into the National Traditional Country Music Hall of Fame. Soon after that honor, Jim was inducted into the West Virginia Music Hall of Fame, where he shares space with Kathy Mattea and Bill Withers. In a framed photo at the top of an overloaded bookshelf, Jim was standing under bright blue stage lights, wearing a tuxedo that seemed as ill-suited as a bullfighter's costume. It was a rare undamaged artifact amid the clutter. Most everything else seemed to hearken back to Jim's childhood, the era of typewriters, homemade shelving, and hand-lettered signage, when hoarding was the only way to protect personal effects from oblivion.

We ambled back up the hill. Jim walked me into the Troubadour Bar & Lounge, which at midafternoon was completely empty but still seemed to breathe. An unbroken collage of fading celebratory Polaroids covered every wall—hundreds of bleary, joyful faces mugging and hugging, a walk-in scrapbook. The only light came from strings of mini holiday bulbs running along the ceiling. They soaked everything in warm red and blue and green, like an LED womb. As if reading my mind, Jim said, "That's how you can tell a redneck: we never take the Christmas lights down." He growled and jabbed my ribs.

A handful of Formica tables were arranged between two sets of maroon vinyl booths, with a small stage up front. On the wall behind the stage hung a life-size Patsy cutout, a massive framed headshot, and one of her gold records, a gift from her widower, Charlie Dick. At the opposite end of the room were the bar and kitchen. Right by the entrance, next to a couple older wooden shelves that held Patsy shirts, Troubadour Studios CDs, and some spare peppers and tomatoes from Jim's garden, was a yellowed Coca-Cola bar sign with a grave warning:

ATTENTION

ALL TROUBLE MAKERS WILL

BE TRAMPLED BEATEN AND

STABBED ALL SURVIVORS

WILL BE PROSECUTED

NO PROFANITY

"Got you a booth," Jim said, leading me up to a table. He wasn't one for sitting down, so I took a seat and watched as the folks arrived. It started slow, a couple regulars who went right up to the bar to give Bertha, Jim's wife of nearly forty years, a hug before the door even had a chance to squeak shut behind them. Bertha had small eyes and a flat mouth that curled into a subtle smile. She hugged with her whole body, eyes closed, her chin resting on her friends' shoulders and her hands firm against their backs, like she was trying to absorb them. When they separated she kept hold of their arms, looking her friends over one more time, then her smile finally opened up all the way. The visitors turned and came over to their booth, easing down like the cushions were their own living-room sofa after a double shift.

Two more couples came in and repeated the same scene before a young waitress walked over to my table and announced it was steak night. Three minutes later I had a frosted mug of beer. Five minutes after that, a plastic plate with a medium-rare slab of beef, fat still dancing from the grill fire. Jim was everywhere, greeting everybody and catching them up on his health problems. Right as he walked past the door, a young blond guy in farm boots and a black T-shirt bounded in, seized Jim's right shoulder, and cried out lovingly, "How ya doin', badass?" then strode right over to a bar stool, all in one unbroken motion. Bertha put a Bud Light in front of him and he drained half of it in one go.

The music was on, classic stuff: George Jones, Kitty Wells, Buck Owens, Ray Price, Tammy Wynette. Fridays are karaoke night, so a loud and twangy-sounding man named Donny, Jim's partner in Troubadour Radio, was busy setting up his DJ rig. The place was beginning to buzz. A crowd of seven middle-aged women from Westminster, Maryland, not far from where I grew up, came in giggling.

"We're having a girls' retreat in Berkeley Springs," one of them told me. "Hotel told us about this place."

"We're here to drink!" shouted one of her friends, and the whole table erupted. The waitress delivered them two pitchers and a tray of frosted mugs.

Donny's wife, a silver-haired woman in a tie-dyed T-shirt with a huge wolf's head across the front, kicked off karaoke. She had an unmade-up moon face and worn, white sneakers, but she absolutely owned Loretta Lynn's "You Ain't Woman Enough (To Take My Man)," wagging a finger and throwing a hand on her hip whenever she landed the chorus. For her final note she threw her head back, eyes closed, and took it all home with a flip of her hair. Then she came off the stage and smiled bashfully while the room went nuts.

No one could match her, though there was no shortage of musical passion in the Troubadour that night. One older man, sitting in the front row all night with only his wife, wobbled up onstage and draped his massive body over a chair by the monitor. Then he started into a version of "Ring of Fire" so tuneless and heaving that I wondered if he'd even heard the original song. He sat motionless on the chair, staring deadpan into the monitor, delivering his lines like a police chief naming casualties at a press conference. In the middle of the song, Jim came over and sat down at my table.

"Got a big boy up there, don't we?" he asked over the din. I said he was certainly putting in the effort.

"Some people just need to get it out," Jim said.

"Ring of Fire" ended, and our colossal singer's wife applauded loudest of all as he exited the stage stone-faced and returned to their table like he'd just completed an honorable, ugly job that only he could do. Another huge man, this one just tall, got up from an otherwise empty booth near the back of the room and sang a more contemporary song I didn't recognize. It was a ballad, and he gave it everything. Eyes closed, two hands on the mic, he lent his unpracticed but orotund baritone to an overwrought tune about Jesus. He died on the cross, I'm worthless without him—the works. It was genuinely touching, but the people had come for beer and a party. We clapped, but we wanted something to scream about.

Donny obliged. Up next, he sang a song about farts, to which he'd added a few appropriate sound effects and choreographed

11

a whole routine where he'd point the microphone at his own ass and let it finish every other line. He had the faces—pained, surprised, relieved, overjoyed—to match the panoply of squeals, wet blasts, and foghorns that he'd programmed in. Later in the night he sang a solemn, reverent version of "That Ragged Old Flag."

At one point, I scanned the room and couldn't see Jim. He wasn't at the bar, near the door, or being toasted at one of the booths. Feeling a little beer-weary, I stepped outside to see if he'd gone out to have his customary evening bourbon. But it was too dark for that. The parking lot was pitch black except for the floodlight above the Troubadour entrance and the red neon coming out of the game room out back. The air had picked up a slight mountain chill. I wondered if he'd actually gone home, to bed; his front door was barely a hundred feet away. But there were only two burly guys out there smoking cigarettes and talking about their motorcycles. Beyond them, there was nothing but black sky and a thin ribbon of Christmas lights on the roadside fence.

But the lights—they moved. Something unseen, on the other side of the gravel lot, shook them loose and a strand fell suddenly to the ground. I walked past the cars, out of reach of the floodlight and the neon, until he finally came into focus. I saw the blue baseball hat in the dim holiday glow.

"Jim?"

"I'm all right," he croaked. "Fixing these lights."

I walked over and saw he was standing in a shallow notch in the grass by the roadside, on the parking-lot side of the fence near the welcome sign. His knees were locked and he was checking on a bulb that had gone out.

"You have to get back in there," I said, the only thing I was sure of.

"I ain't been gone long. One of these bulbs here. See it?" He slipped a little—his Velcro shoe slid down the grass, and he grabbed the fence before anything else happened. Out of nowhere, a pickup truck came over the ridge and roared past us. The air shook as it flew by. Jim didn't look at me. A muffled burst of laughter drifted over from the bar.

"What are you out here for? Why does this need to be done?" I thought of his brother, who'd already seemed annoyed by my showing up in the afternoon. How would he react if Jim dropped dead in my presence by the side of the road, tending to a single expired bulb in the darkness?

"I'm just piddlin'. That's all I do now. Can't do any real work. Fell down in my garden last week and had to wait an hour till the boy came by. He was in Afghanistan, now he helps me with things around here a few days a week. But I can't sit still. I got to keep doing my little chores, my little fixes. You know: piddlin'."

"Well I can't leave you out here. Can't do that to Bertha." After a few seconds he silently draped the rope of lights back over the fencepost and reached out for my arm.

When we got back inside, Donny was at the mic, announcing the winner of a raffle. He pulled a ticket from a hat, read the numbers slowly, and when he finished, the young man at the bar, Mr. How-Ya-Doin'-Badass, slapped the counter and held his latest beer up high.

"Ten pounds of bacon!" Donny said. "Breakfast at your place tomorrow." As our winner walked up through the main room to claim his prize from a cooler onstage, Donny called up another singer. The night wore on. Song after song about pride, loss, God's might, revenge, survival, and love. Each one was a celebration, even the sad ones. Especially the sad ones. In my booth between performances, I read a few of the newspaper clippings that lined the wall, most of which were paeans to the Troubadour by small-town newspaper reporters who'd driven in from three states away and marveled at the throwback charm of it all. Even in the 1980s and 1990s, they all marveled at the "last of the breed." The Troubadour, they all exclaimed, was the kind of place your grandparents would have loved. But this seemed off to me now. Even though past relics and memories filled every visible corner of the place, there was nothing backward-looking about the scene that night. This wasn't a reenactment or the last of anything. People there had come because it was a good time, not because it was a connection to their older relatives. The Troubadour still lived, still performed its role in the present tense. Being there felt like a gift.

For her next song, Donny's wife gave her husband a nod and he cued up that familiar twinkling piano line: "Crazy." People leapt to their feet. One of the Westminster women literally howled. We all mouthed the words but let Donny's wife — I would learn later, while drunkenly thanking her for this performance, that her name was Gay — do her thing. This was deep, mountain-bred soul singing, honed by years of joyful practice. Gay must have been in her early fifties; assuming she'd been singing "Crazy" for about as a long as she could talk, that meant she'd been feeling this song and growing with it for quite a bit longer than Patsy walked the earth. She sang like "Crazy" was in her DNA. For three minutes she was the greatest performer alive. I watched with gratitude, certain that the Troubadour was the center of the world.

Eighty years earlier, no one would have thought that Highland Ridge was the center of anything. It was just a sparsely populated hill with a few families, plenty of sunlight, and spectacularly fertile dirt. The flatter land around Winchester was the biggest apple territory in the United States, possibly the world, and every mountaintop family had a few fruiting trees on their property for cider. But the real ridge crop was tomatoes, which sprang from the soil in a rainbow of colors, growing heavy and firm enough to bend vines and overtake gardens. Jim was the oldest of six children born to Peter Wesley McCoy and his wife, Carrie Virginia Henry McCoy, and he helped his parents deliver the summer crop to the canning facilities that dotted the mountains. As a young man he washed cans for Highland Tomatoes, his grandfather's business. Then the blight arrived. The McCoys and their neighbors moved on to a steadier crop: timber.

The trees came down to fill out the railway lines, the nearest of which went south into downtown Winchester. Working for Guy Spriggs, a former Morgan County sheriff, Jim helped saw, sand, and transport the logs, then held the spikes as his father hammered the tracks into the countryside. It was a small life, demanding and scarcely profitable, but it had its luxuries: fresh vegetables, endless cider, and friends to share them with. The McCoy home was a broad two-story wood box with a long porch and plenty of windows. It was filled at all times with the screech and rumble of six children and frequent visitors, and with the tinny, otherworldly warble of a windup Victrola and a battery-powered radio in the parlor—the electric towers hadn't yet reached Highland Ridge.

The voices and melodies that floated out from those primeval machines were the first proof that Jim McCoy ever had of life beyond hilltop manual labor. He heard mostly hillbilly music, the string-band harmony songs that sounded immemorial: "Wildwood Flower," "Keep on the Sunny Side," "You Are My Sunshine." Somehow, he knew he was going to play them himself.

There was only one person in the McCoy family orbit who actually knew what to do with a guitar: a neighbor named Pete Kelly who made his living cutting stone and building walls. If you entered Winchester from the north on Route 522, as all Berkeley Springs residents did, you passed by a long, waist-high barrier wall that Pete constructed around a commercial apple facility. It still stands. But Pete also liked the McCoys' cider, and during one of his regular visits he taught Jim how to tune a guitar and pluck out a few chords. He gave the boy a week to master "You Are My Sunshine," and came back to find that Jim had done just that. Peter McCoy soon bought his son a guitar from the Montgomery Ward catalogue, an uncommon expense for mountain families, and Jim now had a vision of life beyond a crosscut saw.

He played his first gig at the Berkeley Springs Castle, a private mansion downtown, a few years after World War II. He was paid all of $2, which he gave back to his family in full. But despite the humble debut, the mid-1940s was an auspicious time to enter country music. The war had forced hundreds of thousands of young men from all corners of the United States to live together in close quarters. Naturally, they shared music, and many of them were exposed to real country for the first time in barracks throughout Europe. They returned home with broadened musical tastes, then the GI Bill and urban employment beckoned rural men into cities. This sudden growth and shuffling of the country fan base affected the very sound of the music as well. Before the Depression, there was hillbilly music and there was Western, for the mountain man and the cowboy respectively; Hill & Range, the publisher for Elvis's early repertoire, was named for this dichotomy. After the war it all began blending together, traveling along America's growing network of radio stations and highways, colliding in cities that were filling with victorious soldiers whose roots were in the hills, plains, and deserts. This new strain required a new name.

The term "honky-tonk" stretches back to the late nineteenth century, though it became most commonly associated with highway-set beer joints in post-Prohibition Texas. On the outskirts of oil towns, often near a county line to accommodate changing liquor laws, all manner of little venues sprung up around the state: dance halls, working-class bars, nightclubs, social dens. They proliferated even faster as the military men came home. Their unifying elements were neon lights and music, whether by jukebox or live band. This was a louder setting than country music was used to (Glen Campbell would later refer to these venues as "fighting and dancin' clubs"), and the musicians needed to be heard above breaking bottles, bawdy talk, and brawls. They plugged in and hired drummers, but the move indoors also meant that the tried and true lyrical themes—the family Bible, outdoor work—were replaced by the tribulations of the nightlife: romance, heartbreak, alcoholism, and financial woes. Honky-tonk was the first de-regionalized country music. It was born on the nation's nascent highways, and animated by the struggles of displaced rural people. Hank Williams was the patron saint of this era, and he naturally wrote a song called "Honky Tonkin'," a celebration of aimless club-hopping and drinking that had no wildwood flowers or sweet hills of Virginia in sight: "We're goin' to the city, to the city fair/If you go to the city, you will find me there."

Besides Hank, nobody embodied this relative cosmopolitanism better than Ernest Tubb, "the Texas Troubadour." Tubb started out in the 1930s as a disciple of the great hillbilly yodeler Jimmie Rodgers, but emerged as the quintessential road-warrior bandleader through years on the Lone Star circuit and beyond. His string of hits began with "Walking the Floor Over You" in 1941, and his touring band had drums, electric guitars, and a rollicking sense of swing. They dressed in sharp matching suits and big cowboy hats and boots, the perfect mix of regional affectation and citified flair. Tubb himself never sang beautifully, but over the years he employed some of the most virtuoso musicians to ever play country, including guitarist Leon Rhodes and pedal steel visionary Buddy Emmons, who literally built new gears and components into his instrument in order to make it more amenable to harmonically complex genres, including jazz. Tubb found unprecedented commercial success: radio dominance, a sponsorship by Gold Chain flour, even a headlining spot on a country show at Carnegie Hall in 1947.

By that point, Jim McCoy had already met Ernest Tubb and become completely enthralled. Jim bought Tubb's records, like the guitar, from Montgomery Ward, and then at age fourteen he hitchhiked to Conococheague Park in Hagerstown, Maryland, to see the Texan play. Once they met, Jim started sending letters. By the time he finished high school, Jim was pen pals with one of the biggest stars in country. His insider knowledge and professional connections made him a natural, authoritative DJ, first in Hagerstown and then at WINC, the still-operational Winchester radio station that started broadcasting in 1946. WINC was only the second FM signal in Virginia, broadcasted with a 3-kilowatt transmitter and a 148-foot cloverleaf antenna set up on a hill. On Saturday mornings, Jim hitchhiked down the mountain to host the station's sole country show from 4:30 to 9 a.m.

It was in that capacity, in 1948, that he first met Patsy. He was nineteen and she was three years younger. Jim offered local and touring acts the chance to play on-air for $2, but Patsy didn't even have that. She auditioned for him in the hallway, an *a cappella* take on "San Antonio Rose," and Jim immediately let her sing to the live mic, free of charge. This episode has since become a key component of Patsy lore—her creation myth in a sense. But more important, it inaugurated fifteen years of intense friendship and musical affinity. Jim played guitar for Patsy on many early occasions, became lifelong friends with her second and final husband, Charlie Dick, and eventually served as a pallbearer at her funeral. Jim will tell you how sexy she was, but they were never romantically involved. His love for her was a deeper and purer thing.

Imagine you were a teenage country obsessive from the Depression-era sticks who thumbed rides in the weekend predawn just to play records for fruit pickers. Imagine loving country music that much, and then being tracked down by this disarming, ruby-cheeked, sixteen-year-old spark plug without even two spare dollars to her name. And when she pleads for thirty seconds of your time you step out into an empty tile hallway and she lets forth with *that voice,* bell-clear and sorrowful even as a child. In a few years this voice will sing "Crazy" and the world will fall in love—indeed, the world will have a new musical shorthand for love itself. In that hallway you hear more than just a singer. You hear the future, the shape of your world to come. And as her legend grew after death, you could say with well-earned pride that you were the first person to get behind a radio microphone and fill the airwaves with this stunning voice, the greatest to ever sing country. Imagine all that, and it might make a little more sense why Patsy's face was plastered so persistently all over the Troubadour grounds: on the welcome sign, behind the cash register, and side by side with a picture of Bertha on a shrine-like mantel in the studio.

Jim spent the 1950s rushing from daybreak radio shows to recording sessions and honky-tonk gigs, and he had plenty of fellow travelers. In 1949, the year after Patsy Cline first sang on Jim's Saturday morning show, WINC was one of nearly seven hundred American radio stations that played country. Grand Ole Opry–aping regional radio revues sprung up everywhere from Los Angeles to West Virginia's northern panhandle, where Jim played the *Wheeling Jamboree* concert and radio show for decades. More than sixty full-scale country-themed entertainment parks opened for business during the boom as well. Singers like Gene Autry and Roy Acuff became well-known, diversified businessmen in addition to performers, opening music publishing operations and radio stations. In cities, country TV shows were huge draws and major stops for touring talent. *The Jimmy Dean Show* originated in Washington, D.C., in 1957, and for musicians in the greater orbit of Maryland and the Virginias, that became the grail. Postwar country music was an entrepreneur's playground—the first nationwide American independent music scene. And Jim McCoy tried his hand at every possible opportunity: establishing Troubadour Records and Studios, DJ-ing his radio show, playing gigs whenever possible with the Melody Playboys and as a sideman. There were enough amateur Acuffs like him to scare the mainstream industry into action: in July 1950, Columbia Records became the first label to open a Nashville office and country subsidiary. From that day forward, all those state-highway honky-tonk circuits and regional rodeos slowly drained like open veins until the genre's talent and money pooled in central Tennessee.

As a teenager Jim looked up and made eyes with the daughter of a man whose timber he was sawing. She was Marjie, a sweet country girl, and like a finger-snap they were soon married with three children. Throughout the late 1940s and 1950s, Jim would rise to host a WINC show at 4:30, then head to the southeastern corner of town to manage the Montgomery Ward till 5 p.m. He made $40 a week at that job: "Big money."

But he kept up the grueling music schedule on top of it all, making that twelve-hour drive to Nashville often. His archives are filled with hundreds of showbiz photos: Jim in a suit and ten-gallon hat, mugging, exhausted-looking but boundless; in a cornpone costume with a one-off redneck comedy gang called the Skillet Lickers; posed behind a radio microphone in a press shot; with his band mates or promoters outside a seemingly in-finite number of local fairs, fund-raisers, radio-station promo-tional gigs, barbecues. And there are smiling photos alongside big stars like Ray Price and Dottie West, too. These people were his friends, his admirers even. He finally made it to the Opry stage in the late 1980s, when he was invited to perform at the memorial for Ernest Tubb. But Jim never left for good. He stayed in the upland Shenandoah, and held on as a regional ra-dio star and record producer for decades. The Troubadour, espe-cially for a first-time visitor, feels purely valedictory, a monument to a life lived in noble service to music. But the music Jim lived for is the genre of heartaches, setbacks, and lonely, regret-filled nights. Honky-tonk country is the sound of rural-rooted people taking their first difficult, stumbling steps toward the city, and it is not often the music of triumph. The songs are short, direct, and comfortingly formulaic, but the words, like the backstories of many of the music's stars, continually remind us: life is not a song.

The day after karaoke night, Jim opened Troubadour Park for the summer season. More than two hundred people paid their requested $10 donation for the privilege of setting their foil-covered side dish on the long picnic tables near the giant smoking pistol. One man, his skin as deeply textured as a piece of sunparched oak, carried an enormous macaw on his shoulder as he walked through the crowd. He made his way to the outside bar and paid for one Mountain Dew and a Styrofoam cup full of ice, then took a seat at a white plastic table and poured his soda. As the bubbles fizzed in the sun, the parrot gingerly dismounted from the man's shoulder and put his beak in the cup, guzzling.

By the bar, under a low canopy, Jim and Bertha's employees prepared the smorgasbord. A young man with sweat beading on his downy mustache unscrewed the top from a gallon jug of Great Value original barbecue sauce as the propane grills roared nearby. I recognized him as our steak chef from the night before, and he obviously had the same fuss-free way with chicken. He tipped the jug onto a pile of thighs and legs that he'd arranged in an aluminum tray, then tossed them all with his bare hands, getting sauce up to the T-shirt tan lines above his elbows. Piece by piece he threw the meat on the grill and each time a fresh gust of smoke and burned corn syrup filled the air.

Jim was seated by the donation bucket at the entranceway, greeting everyone who came in. He stayed glued to a stool, giving thumbs up and accepting kisses on the cheek. After a while, Jim's doctor, Matt Hahn—who was spoken of in grateful, hushed tones by the assembled crowd—got on the stage and tapped the mic as Donny turned the volume on. Hahn was in his early fifties but looked like a fresh-faced teenager even with his shaved head. He winced from a blast of feedback.

"Back at the Troubadour!" Hahn announced, to scattered applause. "Let's give a hand to Jim and Bertha. I've had so much fun here I feel bad for all the people who have to live somewhere else. I know the food is about to come out and we'll all get started, but first I wanted to remind everyone that Jim and Bertha have had their problems lately. Lots of doctor's bills, though we know they're going to get better."

Little Eddie, Jim and Bertha's indefatigable busboy, began to unwrap the foil from the dozens of Pyrex dishes at the base of the megagun. The macaw fished zealously for a piece of ice in its soda cup. Its owner had ripped the cup down to a quarter of its original height so the bird could still reach its prize. Rings of carefully manicured Styrofoam were gathered underneath his lawn chair, floating like bubbles in the curling mountain grass. The darkening clouds moved regally, like galleons in full sail.

"And I know we all feel deeply grateful to these people who have given us so many wonderful afternoons like this up here, surrounded by friends and great music," Hahn continued. "So I encourage everyone to visit that donation bucket and see how generous you feel today."

To his right the plywood outdoor restrooms sat empty, their doors slightly ajar. The light still glowed in the men's. To Hahn's left, three children shook the thin frame of a swing-set with chipped paint. There was a small boom as Hahn clicked off the mic, then Donny faded in a Kenny Chesney CD and the lines began forming by the plastic cutlery. A breeze flew in, caramelized chicken and cool pine. The beer-can bin was just full enough to rattle each time a new empty dropped in. Anxiety felt impossible, at least for all but one of us.

Up through a twisting aisle of lawn chairs and crossed legs, a man in a gleaming white cowboy hat strode determinedly toward Jim. He was late thirties, hairless except for a struggling blond goatee. He wore a black sleeveless T-shirt, seemingly ironed, which he had tucked into his Wranglers and secured with a belt buckle big enough for a Buick's hood. It featured a soaring eagle made of polished silver. Behind him, following his stiff black cowboy boots, was a young girl, maybe fourteen and not at all graceful. Poor posture, crimped hair arranged to purposely obscure her face, she wore boys' gym socks pulled up to her knees and black low-top Chuck Taylors that she'd scrawled on with colored pens. A silent older man, presumably her father, trailed her at a small distance.

"Mr. McCoy," the goateed cowboy said, leaning into a conversation between Jim and two older women. The women wrapped up with a kiss on Jim's cheek and went to grab a spot in line. Jim looked up and said nothing.

"Mr. McCoy, I have someone here who I really think you'd like to hear sing."

"Do ya?" Jim asked, skeptical.

"Name's Melanie." He turned and gestured the poor girl in. A thick barbecue din filled the air—screams, laughter, echoing music, monotone debates over the approaching clouds. "She lives out in Great Cacapon, loves to sing. Loves it. I was hoping you might have her onstage tonight and see if she's ready to record."

Jim looked at her with interest but without leering. He was assessing honestly: is this young lady ready for show business?

"What do you sing?" he asked her.

"I like . . ." Her agent's face was so grimly focused you'd think guns were drawn. "Miranda Lambert?" she finally asked.

"Oh, I don't know if these fellas are going to know something that new," said Jim, gesturing to the quartet of road warriors currently setting up and tuning onstage. Guitar, drums, bass, two mics. A couple ponytails. "Anything a little older?"

Stammering but brave, the girl opened her mouth and stared at the agent for approval as the syllables came out slowly.

"Loretta Lynn?"

"They might know that," said Jim. Nodding with approval, he began shuffling up through the chairs, toward the stage, to tell the band they were featuring Melanie on a couple tunes today. They all shook her hand excitedly while the agent placed a gentle palm on Jim's hunched back and said, "We do appreciate this, Mr. McCoy."

Great Cacapon is another one of those tiny towns that dot the panhandle, places that years ago had their own Elks Lodge or roadhouse where Joltin' Jim and the Melody Playboys might play with the local high school surf-rock band. Today, fewer than four hundred people live there. Maybe that man heard Melanie singing with her friends while they watched a music video on a phone. Maybe she was in the church choir. Maybe she was his niece. However it happened, one day he heard her voice and thought: *That could be it.* This girl might sing well enough to get some attention, and who knows what might come of that. Maybe a little money. Maybe a lot of money. Plenty of girls just like her, from nothing-doing towns in the far corners of rural states, have sung their way to fame and wealth. And what do you know, the man who discovered the best there ever was, the real Joltin' Jim McCoy himself, is right up the mountain. Why not dream? It's happened before.

2

*

A Closer Walk with Thee

JUST PAST NOON ON A Saturday in early March, the
first warm weekend of the year, the only sound on South Kent
Street was a screen door slapping behind two teenage girls as
they crossed a short lawn. In black hoodies and tight, neon-
highlighted ponytails, the pair turned and walked behind the
yellow house they had come out of, possibly headed for the shallow creek just past the rear property line, or maybe to the train
tracks beyond that.

The sidewalks were cracked and shifted on South Kent Street.
The porches were peeling. Sixty years ago, the residents of this
gently hilly enclave on the east side of Winchester were strictly
white working class. That Saturday morning, I saw mostly black
families attending to weekend chores, though each house still
looked like a place where money had to stretch. All except for

number 608, which looked even nicer than it did when the street was only white folks. That warm morning, a small crowd had gathered outside, and JudySue Huyett-Kempf was smiling anxiously as she shook hands on the porch, welcoming everyone to the former home of one of the best-known singers in the world.

Not long before, the Patsy Cline Historic House and Museum had been in total disrepair, stuck in legal limbo after decades as a rental. But in 2011, this tin-roofed two-story with white paint and black shutters was transformed into the only tourist attraction in sight. Its five front windows now gleamed like a grand piano, and clean bricks lined its stretch of the sidewalk, engraved with donors' names. Visitors from as far away as Australia and Japan had paid their $8 to get inside and see a painstaking re-creation of the building as it was between 1948 and 1957, when Patsy lived there, the longest residence she held during her short life.

Big necklace, big earrings, big smile, and a long leopard-print blouse: JudySue greeted us like a volcano. Every curl of her hair was teased into place and her makeup was flawless. She was 5'2" but she dominated us.

"The big one for me was Erik Estrada," she explained to a couple on the porch. "He was grand marshal of the Apple Blossom Parade a few years ago and he came and visited us. Gave him a free tour, of course." Then she rolled her eyes in an exultantly hubba-hubba gesture that made her guests seize with laughter.

I was part of the noon group. The house is small enough that only so many people can go in at a time, and this weekend was slated to be busier than usual: though the house's official visitor season doesn't start until April, JudySue and her fellow board members of Celebrating Patsy Cline, the 501(c)3 that instigated the house's resurrection, had opened it that week to mark the fiftieth anniversary of the deadly plane crash that ended Patsy's life. They were hosting tours of the house all day Saturday, followed by a party downtown that evening and a graveside memorial service just outside town on Sunday morning, the actual date of the tragedy.

JudySue opened the front door and the air changed immediately. The wood-box television and 45 player in one corner were the only traces of halfway modern technology in the living room. Otherwise there were only black and white photos, a white upright piano near the front window, and a side table next to a floral print couch draped with homemade lace. A framed copy of Patsy's most famous early '60s headshot, signed to her mother ("We finally made it!"), sat prominently on the piano lid. Three departing Patsyphiles were talking with an impeccably groomed man in white gloves, one of a handful of docents leading visitors through the house.

"Those were actually Patsy's," JudySue beamed, pointing to a group of matching salt and pepper shakers on the kitchen windowsill, a small portion of the singer's sizable collection. "And same with the table and chairs right near 'em." She had a right to be proud: In the Lazarus tale of 608 South Kent Street, JudySue was Jesus. Its reopening was the signal achievement of her twenty-year campaign to make Winchester synonymous with Patsy, or at least to recognize her existence at all. JudySue's struggle in this effort shocks most outsiders. After all, most little-known hamlets would be thrilled to capitalize on a hometown girl of such eminence: the first solo female inductee to the Country Music Hall of Fame and one-time subject of a U.S. postage stamp, with a continually replenished fan base to rival Sinatra's. She even sang at Carnegie Hall and got a posthumous star on the Hollywood Walk of Fame. But Patsy Cline didn't belong to the Winchester elite when she lived here, and not even her tragic death and subsequent global stardom ever earned their affection.

Patsy was at the height of her fame, only thirty years old with two young kids, when she boarded a single-engine Piper Comanche that her tourmates had affectionately dubbed "the shitbox." It was March 5, 1963, and she was heading home to Nashville after a show. The plane's nickname, like Jim McCoy's touring hearse, was a bit of gallows humor in an industry where performers famously died on the road. Patsy herself had been hospitalized for weeks after a head-on collision about eighteen months earlier. Jim had two of his own death-defying crashes in his touring days. So some of the bigger stars had taken to traveling by plane. It seemed safer.

Around sunrise the plane clipped the top tier of the woods near Camden, Tennessee, and plummeted. The crash was horrific: the plane looked shredded, the contents strewn all through the site. As one friend noted grimly, "Very little of her came back to Winchester." But thousands of heartbroken fans and friends made the trip to Virginia for the funeral. Many called it the saddest day they ever experienced, but the *Winchester Star*—then as now the city's only newspaper—described the solemn event as "a mob scene . . . They acted as if it was a 'dollar day' at the department store."

"David will be leading your tour," JudySue said, then called over the man in white gloves. "You're in luck." She stepped away into the kitchen, where she'd converted one built-in shelf to a gift shop.

"Where you folks from?" David asked. One man was from northern Virginia, another from central Pennsylvania. They were both over fifty, alone, just big-time Patsy fans looking to experience the house. Neither literally wore his fandom like the couple from Ohio whose Patsy T-shirts, with her mile-wide smile and full cheeks, peeked out from underneath their Steelers windbreakers.

David gave us the facts of her early life, which had been most rigorously detailed in *Patsy Cline: The Making of an Icon,* written and published by Celebrating Patsy Cline historian Douglas Gomery a few years earlier. She was born Virginia Patterson Hensley in 1932, the first child of a sixteen-year-old mother and forty-three-year-old father. "Ginny" spent her first two years living with her mother, Hilda Hensley, in a wooded cabin without electricity or plumbing. Hilda grew vegetables in a garden behind the house and caught fish in the nearby Shenandoah River. Patsy's father, Sam Hensley, worked construction and hauling jobs throughout Virginia before landing a salaried position as head boilerman for Washington and Lee University. The family moved with him to Lexington and was housed in a relatively luxurious home in the woods near the gymnasium. For five years, Ginny sat by her bedroom window and heard weekly dance concerts by the world-class jazz orchestras that came to campus for fraternity mixers. That was 1937 to 1942, the height of the big-band era. It was the first professional music that Ginny ever heard.

David narrated this tale with such practiced earnestness that it was hard to tell if he actually liked Patsy or was simply an expert salesman. At the end of an anecdote about her childhood bout with rheumatic fever, an experience that nearly left her voiceless, he intoned, "Imagine, a world without Patsy's voice," and then let a moment of solemn silence go by. Our Ohio couple nodded in unison.

He omitted, however, the worst of Patsy's ordeals: Sam's sexual abuse, the extent of which will likely never be known. Biographers (Gomery is the third so far) mention her occasional crying bouts to close friends as an adult. Late nights on tour, a thousand miles from her children, she'd occasionally just weep. Sloppy, tortured crying, full of self-hatred but never confessional. No one can corroborate it now. But for what it's worth, Hilda and Sam divorced shortly after the family achieved some measure of stability upon moving into the South Kent Street house.

Hilda and Patsy moved nineteen times in the sixteen years leading up to their arrival on South Kent, sometimes with Sam but often without. They were determined to provide a proper, stable home for Patsy's much younger siblings, Sylvia and Sam Jr. They had no money. Patsy dropped out of high school and worked hourly jobs around the city, at the movie theater snack bar or a chicken slaughterhouse. Her longest job was at Gaunt's Drug Store, about a ten-minute walk southwest. She was a beloved soda jerk who memorized everyone's orders and even served black customers more than a decade before Virginia desegregated its schools. In the evenings and weekends she sang anywhere people would listen—every beery, nicotine-stained hellhole and every church social too.

But rarely in Winchester. There was no country scene in her hometown beyond Jim McCoy's radio show, no love for mountain culture or cowboy couture. So among the city's patrician class Patsy was known simply as a loudmouth and unregenerate flirt. She called out to passersby from her porch swing and sang at disreputable venues with all-male bands. She had a deadbeat father and a divorced mother, and didn't even have the decency to feel ashamed of herself.

Worse still: She wore pants.

In the small parlor, where the family's dinner table stood on a rug made from patches of World War II army uniforms, rested a bona fide breathtaker for Patsy fans: a replica of the blue-and-white tasseled cowgirl dress that she wore in her early career. In pictures with other women of the time, Patsy always looks bigger, less dainty, and yet this dress was positively petite. It hung starkly on a vintage dress-form mannequin next to Hilda's sewing machine, the family's main source of income during their years on South Kent. Hilda was a master seamstress and made all of Patsy's early outfits by hand. She also sewed and repaired clothes for Winchester's upper class and babysat their children. A kids' toy made from wooden spools and red thread dangled from the Singer.

We followed David up the narrow, creaking stairs by the front door and into the bedroom, which was even starker than the lower floor. Sam Jr.'s bed was hidden behind a sheet on a rope line. On the other side was Patsy's bed, and another where Sylvia slept with Hilda.

Singing was "the one thing she could do that wasn't going to cost us," Hilda later said. Patsy got her first real break at age twenty, playing with a regional country bandleader named Bill Peer, who was married and a father but still fell in love with her. It was Peer who suggested she call herself Patsy, from her middle name, Patterson. Their affair was well known and whispered about, and the indignity probably pushed her toward Gerald Cline, the twenty-eight-year-old heir to a construction fortune who wooed her whenever the Peer group stopped at the Moose Lodge in Brunswick, Maryland. They married in 1953, then fought bitterly for years because she refused to stay off the road and have children. By 1956 Patsy had split from Peer, then from Cline, but had fought her way onto a regular spot on Jimmy Dean's television variety show, filmed in Washington, D.C. Camera-trained, she then auditioned for *Arthur Godfrey's Talent Scouts,* one of the most popular television shows in the country. A win on Godfrey's heavily sponsored program could make a career, and that's what happened for Patsy when she sang her third single, "Walkin' After Midnight," in early 1957. The impressed host deemed it a "wam-doodler" on-air.

The single sold well enough that Hilda could move the family to a bigger house down the street, number 720, and rent number 608 for extra cash. The *Winchester Star* wrote up the performance but misspelled Patsy's name and called the song "I Walk Alone at Midnight."

But before any of that, before the television appearances and hit singles, there was this low-ceilinged bedroom, bisected by a thinning sheet on a rope. The lower floor was for entertaining, which Patsy and Hilda did whenever possible. But the bedroom, with its close quarters and drafty windows, embodied more of what those uncertain years must have felt like. Humiliation—suffering it and conquering it—was the grand tragic theme of Patsy Cline's life, and this bedroom was the only half-private space she had throughout her leanest years. It was where she made her face up and prepared for late nights that she hoped might free her from such a hectic, needy existence. A blanket on the foot of Patsy's bed was the actual handmade quilt she slept with. The glove box by Sam Jr.'s bed—Patsy was a glove collector, never without multiple pairs—was also genuine. The place felt heavy.

"I hope you guys feel some of what we feel up here every day," David said, making eye contact with each member of the group one by one. A drawl seeped into his voice, barely perceptible. "I know there's something here. I work here a lot by myself, sometimes the entire day. And I hear things. And I think, 'OK, did I not get enough sleep?'" He laughed and so did everyone else, secure that he wasn't just some nut. Then he quickly regained his composure.

"But I've heard the door close up here a few times." No one laughed.

Saturday night, my tie and jacket on, I walked over to the posh, boxy George Washington Hotel, one of downtown Winchester's dueling monoliths along with the regal Handley Library on the other end of Piccadilly Street. The main street's name was one tip-off that Winchester, like many early-American cities, owed a lot of its physical and historical character to England: the skinny streets were lined with brick and stone, accented with black metal gates and vines crawling up every downspout. The library's tall columns and green metal roof would have looked familiar to the pigeons of Trafalgar Square.

Even the hotel's name was a nod to British roots. Washington lived in town back when he commanded troops for the queen. In 1755, he was tasked with leading a Winchester-based regiment in the French and Indian War, and it nearly drove him to despair. In this "cold and barren frontier," as he called it, Washington fought constantly with his soldiers over their alcoholism and laziness. He promised fifty lashes for men caught drinking in town, and hanged one attempted deserter. He threatened to resign less than two months after arriving. But years later, when Washington was living far away and campaigning for the Virginia House of Burgesses, he returned to Winchester on election day and handed out wine, brandy, beer, cider, and rum punch from a wagon in the center of town. He won in a landslide. It was his first political victory.

In 2013, there was still a persistent divide between folks who could be wooed by free booze and those who could afford to offer it. The stately stone hotel charged the highest rates for the nicest room in town, yet from its sidewalk I could see around the corner to the Royal Lunch, the platonic ideal of a dive bar that surely would have been a favorite of Washington's ungovernable platoon had they lived to see the Bud Light era. In one sense, the Royal Lunch was just the townie bar, and the hotel the yuppie tourist haven. But their proximity spoke to Winchester's almost elemental schizophrenia. On the walk over from 608 South Kent, I passed by two cemeteries, one Confederate and the other Union, that stare at each other from opposite sides of the street. It is said that Winchester switched sides more than seventy times during the Civil War, and a major highway nearby is still named for Jubal Early, the Confederate general who lost the Third Battle of Winchester in 1864. Standing in the road was like staring at the brain lobes of an entire town. The Union cemetery was compact and geometric—all straight lines, untouched by heathenish creativity. The identical, undecorated stones were packed like ice cubes in their tray. Across the street, the Confederate site's Gothic fence was adorned with wrought-iron wisteria. The burial sites were roomier, the stones varied from soaring columns to squat shelves. This site had stood as a graveyard since the 1840s, but the Civil War–specific portion, named Stonewall Cemetery, was founded by bereaved Winchester women to accommodate the shallowly buried bodies that farmers kept unintentionally disinterring with their tools in the war's aftermath. Eventually, some 2,500 men were reburied in Stonewall. Into the twentieth century, Winchester held an annual Confederate

Memorial Day gathering of somber reflection and song on the grounds.

The George Washington was built in 1924 but closed in the 1970s and was used as an old-age home for a time. Like the Cline House, it had recently been restored, though in the hotel's case the rejuvenators were the not-even-remotely-nonprofit Wyndham Hotel Group, which had installed a loud, low-lit lobby bar with high ceilings and jazz-club décor: the Half Note Lounge. On Saturday night, this was the site of the official memorial-weekend party. The place was buzzing with Patsy fans and Winchesterites who knew her when. JudySue, in a different but even more resplendent outfit, this one accentuated with a turquoise wrap, was drifting through the crowd thanking everyone. Around 8:30, Patsy's daughter, Julie, got up to thank the assembled and say how much it meant to return home. Julie was only four years old when her mother died, and was only beginning to engage publicly as a family representative. She had just earlier that year been sworn in as president of the global Patsy Cline fan club.

"It means so much to have her here," JudySue told me as Julie set down the microphone and everyone quietly applauded. "To have her blessing and her involvement is just . . . so important."

Julie's presence carried so much weight because Winchester remains one of those noble American towns where history can still be felt as a living force. It is spoken of and fretted about like the clouds hovering over the Troubadour. For generations, Winchester chose to see itself as a New World Camelot or Rome — a grand tragic opera of future presidents, wartime heroics, and European fortunes. Against this backdrop, no amount of number-1 records or global adoration could erase the notion that Patsy Cline was just another piece of poor white trash from South

Kent Street. A certain class just never considered her worth acknowledging, and Winchester's ways are so deeply set that that attitude has survived, in an admittedly limited scope, into the twenty-first century. The few nominal public acknowledgments of her connection to the town—a street name, a sign along Interstate 81, a historic marker outside the house—all popped up in the 1980s and later, usually thanks to private backing, and with considerable opposition from the city government in each case. Patsy Cline Boulevard, for example, is an entrance road to the Apple Blossom Mall, not an official street. The government doesn't even have to hold its nose and plow it when it snows.

As it happens, the George Washington Hotel was once an important hub for the nose-holding set. In the 1950s, its lobby restaurant was the main daytime social site for doctors, lawyers, businessmen, and their wives. By night their employees and customers, most of whom lived on Kent Street, descended upon Loudoun Street, a few blocks west. They saw movies or talent shows at the Palace Theatre, got drunk at the bars, or just sat in their parked cars and called out to each other.

Patsy's wedding to Gerald Cline was the closest she got to the proprietary life, and it's easy to imagine her struggling to adapt to its strictures before ultimately embracing the truth: she had to sing. And the best kind of guy to accommodate that dream was a crass, boisterous good ol' boy named Charlie Dick. Like Patsy, he was the oldest of three and never saw his father after the age of fifteen. Also like Patsy, Charlie liked to drink and cuss and fall in love, and they did all three from the moment they met each other on Friday, April 13, 1956. Julie, their first child, was born in 1958.

All around us at the Half Note Lounge, people were growing louder and drinking the night's special, a martini-glass bourbon cocktail called The Cline. Every bartender was visibly frustrated by the recipe, which involved a just-so orange twist. Over at the microphone, a nervy-eyed brunette named Liz Ruffner, Celebrating Patsy Cline's resident tribute singer, cued up her backing tracks on an iPad and performed alarmingly note-perfect renditions of all the hits, including "Walkin' After Midnight," "Strange," and "She's Got You." Her voice was a little huskier than Patsy's but she understood the void in those songs and luxuriated in it. She sang without any outreach to the crowd.

Idling at the bar, I watched two of the younger women in attendance yell warmly at each other over the noise. They were watering down their Clines with Sprite and looked like they'd spent most of their years breathing through cigarettes. The bottle blonde had an ornate tattoo visible across her upper chest, and the brunette, with no tattoos I could see, soon caught me eavesdropping and invited me to the spring Apple Blossom Festival.

"It's amazing. Whole town's just drinking outside for like a week. Like Mardi Gras with apples. I'm gonna have my beads on —she knows!" The blonde laughed and shook her head.

"I love this hotel now," said the brunette. "So classy. Couple years ago this was, like, a mental hospital? Awful. Now you got music and it's beautiful looking. It'll fill up around Apple Blossom.

"This girl right here," she shouted at me, wrapping an unmuscular arm around her drinking partner, "we've known each other forty . . . forty-one?"

"Forty-one," said the blonde.

"Forty-one years. Since we were little kids."

Her friend nodded. "Don't listen to her," she said. "She goes on and on."

That was true. In a raspy, happy voice, the brunette told me that she spent time at a youth home as a teenager. She'd lived in Winchester all her life, and her father used to drink with Patsy. He even claimed that he kissed her once, and so this woman grew up hearing that if Patsy had only been a bit younger, he would have married her instead of the brunette's mother. She watched Julie move around the crowd, signing programs and giving hugs.

"We could be twins!" she shouted, then went back and ordered another drink from the bar that wouldn't have served her grandmother.

The official Celebrating Patsy Cline line on Charlie and Patsy is that they were nothing like the 1985 Patsy biopic *Sweet Dreams*, starring Jessica Lange and Ed Harris. In Winchester, everybody calls that film simply "the movie," and nobody speaks of it fondly. Part of the CPC mission, particularly since Charlie has been generous with his support, is to scrub up the Patsy story for public view. Enough with the hearsay and domestic abuse accusations. As David put it: They fought, sure, but it only got physical one time.

No matter how you frame it, their marriage might be charitably called tempestuous. Their home life was tense when Patsy's career flatlined in the late 1950s, following the success of "Walkin' After Midnight." She continued to record with her regular producer, the visionary "Nashville Sound" pioneer Owen Bradley, but nothing stuck to the charts. They tried everything: mambo and gutbucket country, gospel and weepy pop ballads. Then lightning struck, in the form of "I Fall to Pieces," written by a young Hank Cochran. It was a heartbreak ballad like dozens of others Patsy had already recorded (she called them "hurtin' songs"), and she curled around the melody, tugging at the lyrics with her signature rise-and-fall crying effect. It was released in early 1961, around the time Patsy gave birth to Randy, her second child with Charlie, and the song crawled up the charts all through the summer. Patsy's near-fatal car crash came on June 14, when she was running errands. "I Fall to Pieces" hit number 1 on the pop charts while she convalesced. Tribute performances, many by younger female singers who already considered Patsy an influence, began at the Opry. By the time she got back on the road she was a superstar.

No one was better suited to push country music into the mainstream. Always a powerful belter, Patsy had a busy touring and recording schedule that made her voice even stronger through the late 1950s. She became more expressive with her breaths and vibrato. Bradley brought in Elvis's backing vocalists, the Jordanaires, whose pillowy harmonies grounded Patsy perfectly, like the hazy, distant backgrounds in Looney Tunes clips. Unlike earlier female country singers like Kitty Wells, Patsy had no twang in her voice. It was accentless and firm as copper, the perfect vehicle to advance the gentrification of the genre that started with honky-tonk. Take "Crazy," her second enormous hit, from 1962. Even after decades of overuse in commercials and movies and compilations, it remains miraculous. For something so lonely sounding, it is wildly busy: the melody leaps and skips from high notes to low, under a chord progression that floats mercurially though major, minor, and seventh voicings. It's a classic torch song; it would have fit perfectly on *Sinatra & Strings*, released the same year, and Patsy sings with an emotional depth and technical precision that equal anything her New Jersey contemporary ever accomplished. She makes the hopscotching melody sound restrained and muted. Her low notes are agonizing, her high ones are soaring. She sounds genuinely conflicted and heartbroken—when she gets to "Crazy for feeling so lonely," she drops out for a split second in the middle of the final word, only to reemerge, more powerful and defiant than ever, in the last syllable. Patsy took Hank Williams's despairing yodel and carried it to a new plane. She bridged the gap between "Lost Highway" and Maria Callas.

Even after her fame arrived, Patsy would roll by WINC whenever she came back into town. With her hair in curlers, she'd park her beloved red Cadillac and come inside to cozy up with Jim McCoy on-air and play her new single. For Jim, her success was of course a thrill—his friend and Valley compatriot had made it to Valhalla. Moreover, she was his entry into Nashville, the reason he started going down there regularly and made the friends he made. But Patsy also ushered in the mindset that eventually shut people like Jim McCoy out of national stardom; her success with Bradley opened the floodgates to Nashville, and it became harder than ever for singers to make it elsewhere. Except for the harder-rocking Bakersfield stars like Buck Owens and Merle Haggard, mainstream country music became increasingly gussied-up throughout the 1960s: strings, masterful singing, and expert musicianship became the norm, even for those artists, like Ray Price and George Jones, who were as road-tested and rural-born as they came. The honky-tonk sound began to feel provincial, and Patsy's voice was the one that made it so.

Liz Ruffner cued up the backing track for "True Love" and dedicated it to her parents. A middle-aged woman swayed drunkenly by JudySue, calling out to her tall, bald husband who waved dismissively before turning back to a heated conversation with another man in the doorway. "It's my daddy's birthday," Liz announced, a subtle Valley curl in her vowels. "He passed away many years ago." No one acknowledged her.

When Patsy performed at Carnegie Hall in 1961, as part of a veritable "Grand Ole Opry Goes Manhattan" package concert, the *Winchester Star* only mentioned it on page 7, a week after the show. Right as "I Fall to Pieces" peaked, Patsy returned home for a rare Winchester gig, leading her band atop the movie theater concession stand in between shows. Years later, Jim McCoy recalled to one of her biographers, "the women—it was never the men, that's one thing I'd like to clarify—the women started blowing horns and booing her . . . She started crying so bad . . . she said, 'Why do people in Winchester treat me like this?'"

My new Sprite-guzzling female friends likely knew that feeling, as did many of the people in the Half Note Lounge that night. From the conversations I overheard, they either grew up with Patsy's music playing on a loop throughout their childhoods, or they knew her personally. Their mama knew her mama. They had heard of her legendary friendliness while shopping at Gaunt's. Or in the case of Anita, a middle-aged woman I bumped into while trying to avoid being tackled by the drunken dancer, they heard Patsy sing as a child.

Anita grew up in Frederick County but later moved downtown and had lived there for thirty-four years with her husband, Nathan, who sat next to her, smiling silently. She shared her story as Liz sang the loping gospel standard "Just a Closer Walk with Thee," a live version of which was the final recording Patsy ever made.

"We never were the moneyed people," Anita said of her early life. Her father worked in the city at the employment commission, and her mother held multiple jobs, for a tractor company and then for medical offices.

"My mom was very aware of Patsy Cline, but we never discussed her back then." Anita's aunt and uncle, however, took her to see Patsy perform when she was a little girl. "I remember seeing her, realizing she was so different. She looked a little different; she was more made up than a woman in my family.

"I'll never forget, in 2000, going into a remote little pub in England and Patsy Cline was playing. Then we later had some English friends come over and their high-school-age kids wanted to see Patsy Cline's grave." At the time there was nothing in town to commemorate the singer besides her resting place. But nowadays, Anita said, "We've decided to honor her the way she deserved. It's almost as if we developed a conscience."

By going to college, serving on the Winchester board of education, and participating in state and local political campaigns, Anita found a very different life for herself than her rural upbringing had promised. She still referred to herself proudly as a "county girl," meaning Frederick County, though one of her daughters lived in the Baltimore suburbs and she and Nathan had traveled the country and abroad. In this way, she echoed the postwar experience of the entire Winchester-area middle class, which had generally grown wealthier and achieved agency that their ancestors wouldn't have even dreamed about. But this wasn't because Anita's ilk were invited into the proprietary class; it was a result of the whole class structure shattering altogether. The old local tycoons were less powerful, but corporations like Rubbermaid, Pactiv, and Valley Health, which owns the infinitely expanding Winchester Medical Center on the city's west side, had replaced them. The old restrictions gave way, presenting many rural people with new options in the world, but every year for decades, a town that lived and breathed history had fewer and fewer people for whom that history was actually personal.

The town may have modernized but Patsy Cline's music did not, and so the music became a mainline to the old days. Patsy was on her way up when she died, and she is now preserved as a picture of ascendancy, frozen forever at the moment when a lifetime of spit-upon white-trash struggle finally gave way to upper-class respectability. Her voice is the sound of talent triumphing over despair. Her songs of lost love now signify a lost era, and so they find a new audience every year—ironically, an audience in search of "real" country, or a dose of postwar American optimism and innocence. Patsy is gone from the world, but the world still demands that she perform.

That's why the Half Note bar buzzed with triumph on Saturday night. The descendants of Patsy's people were now in positions of power and influence, free to toast with cocktails in the lobby of the George Washington. And Patsy embodied everything they claimed to value in a person: hard work, generosity, humor, irreverence, and God-given talent. As Liz sang the mournful opening bars of "Crazy," Anita called over her mother, Louise, who worked alongside Patsy at a newsstand in the 1950s. Louise is now a docent at 608 South Kent. I asked her, what caused all this change in Winchester in the last few decades?

Louise looked me straight in the eye and said, almost by angry reflex, "Northerners came in."

A few minutes later, in need of some steadying moonlight, I pushed through the crowd and out the lobby to the George Washington's rear parking lot. I took a seat on the curb without noticing three teenagers hidden in the shadows barely 40 feet away. A girl with a pierced nose and jagged hair was sitting on the curb too, talking tearfully on the phone to someone who had hurt her. Her tears were thick. Her nose dripped snot. "I don't *care!*" she moaned into her phone, then ripped it away from her cheek and looked longingly at the moon, like she wanted it to seize her.

Her confidants were nearby, a boy and girl canoodling in the parking garage light. I figured they'd driven their tortured friend or maybe met her there, in a safe and central place where they wouldn't be noticed. They were pressed so tightly together they were basically wearing each other. When friends rescue you from a morass and then feel each other up in public while you weep at its edge—that's country music. That is life at the border between youthful whimsy and adult despair. This kind of dreadful night is how a person becomes herself, how she decides that a cruel hometown or bad boyfriend don't deserve her. Erase the phone, dirty up the party inside, and this was a scene that Patsy Cline lived more than once.

JudySue insisted on taking me around town on Sunday morning, a few hours before the graveside memorial service. Typically she delivers her "Patsy's Winchester" spiel from the front of a coach bus filled with visiting Patsyphiles. For many years she did it in a full cowgirl outfit. That day she just drove her Camry. It was the first morning of daylight saving time, and downtown was still quiet. But not JudySue.

"This town is all about Washington and the Civil War," she said, as if in judgment of the empty streets. "That's all they care about."

Unlike many of the people who come to Winchester for Patsy tourism, JudySue isn't a lifelong fan. Back when, Patsy was just a singer in the same bars that JudySue went to on Saturday nights with her teenage boyfriend.

"I had no idea," she told me. "I was in my own world then, doing my own thing. I was into Elvis, rock and roll. That's one thing Patsy and I shared—we *loved* Elvis."

JudySue grew up an only child in Berryville, one exit east on the Harry F. Byrd Highway. Her father traveled all over the country training racehorses and then switched careers to work for Canter, an oil business now owned by Southern Energy Company. JudySue would have loved to have been a singer, but had to settle for being Miss Apple Blossom 1961. (She bragged about the accomplishment, but I had to figure out the year for myself later.)

She entered the banking industry early, working her way up over twenty-eight years to branch manager for Winchester Farmers and Merchants. Then, in the early 1990s, her bank was robbed three times in six months. She was a hostage twice, and had her hair pulled at gunpoint. "I had just purchased a gorgeous white suit, and they got it all dirty," she remembered. "That's what really got me upset."

She left banking and began volunteering for the Winchester Tourism Board in 1994. After fielding dozens of calls asking about then-nonexistent Patsy attractions, JudySue petitioned the chamber of commerce to start Celebrating Patsy Cline, which became independent of the chamber four years later. By that time she'd immersed herself in Patsyana and grown amazed that the city was willfully ignoring such a goldmine.

As a rural girl and a female professional in an old-money town, JudySue also grew to appreciate just how daring Patsy was. "She supported her family, she worked, she sang. She was quite a busy lady. They threw things at her, but she got right back up again and kept singing. She was way, way ahead of her time. A woman in a man's world. And she adapted herself to that."

We passed the building where Patsy recorded her earliest sides, then continued on to the Triangle Diner, where she is rumored to have worked. We stopped at Gaunt's Drug Store, which now lacked the sundae bar where Patsy benevolently held court as a teenager, giving out extra toppings even when folks couldn't afford them. In place of ice cream, Gaunt's now housed a storefront and memorabilia counter devoted to her. A life-size painting of Patsy in her trademark red cowgirl dress smiled out from the main window. It bore no resemblance whatsoever.

Gaunt's longtime owner, Harold "Doc" Madagan, began working there shortly after Patsy left. JudySue explained that Doc was threatening retirement, and there were no set plans for the building. She wanted Celebrating Patsy Cline to have it for displaying the original dresses and other clothes that wouldn't be safe from deterioration in drafty 608 South Kent. She sounded anxious but resolved. A McDonald's loomed tauntingly across the parking lot, though even it had bowed to Patsy's legacy: there was a huge wooden 45 record in the window and a couple black and white photos of her hanging near the bathrooms.

JudySue continued on to the improbably regal Handley High School, which has soaring columns and a central football arena befitting a prep school for robber barons' sons. This was the school that Patsy dropped out of; it's possible she didn't attend classes at all. Either way, their new performing arts center, opened in 2011, is named for her.

"Let me show you the rich area," JudySue said, conspiratorially. She took a left turn onto Washington Street, a wide boulevard flanked on both sides by palatial plantation-style homes.

Here were wide, wraparound porches and gilded domes, field-length yards behind walls of manicured hedges.

"This was all lawyers," she explained. "Most are still owned by the original families."

JudySue described Winchester as a place where "you never pay any attention to your neighbor." You keep to yourself and don't question things too much. Unlike Anita and Nathan the night before, JudySue was a longtime member of the city's business class. When you look at the town from an economic perspective, she said, "I wouldn't say things have changed. It's still a tight ship with the city council. Most of them are still there from when I started." I asked for names and she paused for a while, then declined. "I gotta live here."

All nine members of the Celebrating Patsy Cline board were businesspeople: a retired banker, a woman from Valley Health, the downtown development director—people with wealth and connections, but not necessarily members of those original families from Washington Street. The Cline House's thirteen docents were people like David and Louise, fans and contemporaries who just want to spend time in that rarefied air, sharing their love of the singer. The criterion for membership was the same for both positions; everyone had to be "True Patsy," as JudySue described it—warriors, believers, missionaries.

"A lot of the people who come to the house are either from that generation or they have a connection to it," she explained. "They say, 'Oh my mom had a couch like that. My grandma had that plate.' That generation only had each other."

She turned right on Piccadilly Street, headed for the east side of town where South Kent converges with Route 522, the main southbound road. Catty-corner from the George Washington Hotel, a thin café looked squished into position between its neighbors. Its front windows were decorated with a spray-painted name: JUST LIKE GRANDMA'S.

"I don't like that," JudySue said, not quite under her breath. I asked what she meant. "They just opened. It looks a little cheap, doesn't it? They're trying to do something with this block."

I didn't ask her to clarify. The intersection by the hotel was its own kind of microcosm: directly across the street from the hotel, a tall midcentury apartment building with a striking art deco facade loomed, empty and out of business. Large blue sans-serif letters spelled out WINCHESTER TOWERS on its cracked stucco. Across the street, a newly opened tobacconist's shop looked warm and welcoming with stately gold lettering on pristine glass, like every other newly opened tobacconist's shop on earth. What's cheaper looking—a disused historic property, a faceless lifestyle boutique, or a homey diner?

We drove out into the county toward Shenandoah Memorial Park, where the afternoon's service would be held. On that day fifty years earlier, Route 522 was a parking lot for Patsy's funeral. People left their cars sitting there to walk up. But at the moment it just looked like another quiet country highway waiting for its share of sprawl. The farmland rolled by and the houses grew farther apart. We pulled into the parking lot of Omps Funeral Home, right by the park.

JudySue was nervous. She looked over the empty spaces, wondering how many would be filled in a couple hours. Fifty attendees would put her at ease, give her the sense that all the weekend's preparations were worth it. Coverage by the *Star* and by Channel 3, the local TV news, would help the mission as well. But at the moment she had a ghost story on her mind.

It cost $100,000 to refurbish 608 South Kent, and that sum

wasn't easy to raise. The day that Celebrating Patsy Cline got its final $20,000, the house was still only bones: no heat, plumbing, or power. JudySue received the celebratory call just past 6 p.m. She hung up, elated, and then immediately the phone rang again. It was a South Kent Street neighbor calling to tell her that all the lights were on in the house.

"So I drive by, and it's lit up like a Christmas tree. I circle the block, and come back and everything's off again. Now, I don't believe that stuff, but I called the city the next day and they told me, the electricity was off the whole time." She let a silent moment hang in the parked car. Then she sung the descending opening syllables of "Crazy" and laughed to herself.

Well before 3 p.m., more than sixty people had shuffled quietly into the funeral home's main hall and taken the programs David had prepared, featuring dozens of pixelated Patsy photos. A young woman from Channel 3 was sitting near the back with a video camera. The other guests, dressed for church, fiddled with forget-me-not seed packets illustrated with Patsy's portrait that the docents had given out with the programs.

On the other side of the room stood a plain wooden podium, a massive ribbon-adorned wreath of roses, and a large framed photo of Patsy, faded to the point of near invisability. It was in fact the very same photo that had stood on an easel in the exact same spot a half-century earlier. David, who had recently fulfilled a long-held dream and been ordained as a minister, walked up to the podium right on time in a purple clerical scarf.

"Ours is a sacred purpose today," he opened, in a voice indistinguishable from his docent's tone. "Patsy dreamed, she achieved, she overcame." We had gathered to celebrate "a life not forgotten, a voice that cannot be silenced."

I leafed through the program and read one of the two poems David had written for the occasion, "Our Shenandoah Angel": "As you journeyed through life with your head held high,/No one could stop you, no matter how they tried."

The first speaker was current Winchester mayor Elizabeth Minor, a longtime local public servant who had handily won her second term only a few months earlier. In 2010, she designated September 4 as Patsy Cline Day, one of the only official recognitions the singer has ever received from Winchester. Mayor Minor walked slowly to the podium, clutched its sides, looked up at the audience with a distant stare, and began crying immediately.

"To me, anyone that isn't a fan of Patsy Cline is totally un-American," she laughed after pulling herself together. "She is one of Winchester's very own . . . Everywhere you go, everyone knows Patsy Cline, and everyone knows where she's from. She is such a strong part of Winchester's history."

Tracie Dillon, a one-time Celebrating Patsy Cline board member who was born years after the plane crash, tearfully opened her speech with a quote from Harriet Tubman. She called Patsy "my lifelong idol" and said, "She rose above the things that weighed her down, and she proudly proclaimed where she was from, despite being shunned by those who didn't have the same belief in her dream." She then trembled her way through the lyrics of "Always," recorded only a month before Patsy's death: "Days may not be fair, always/That's when I'll be there, always."

Julie, Patsy's daughter, then rose and approached the spotlight once again. "I didn't prepare a big speech," she said, apparently honestly. She had none of the others' stage-readiness or resolve, though I'd never seen such a mixture of grief, joy, and grace in a person's eyes before.

"I guess you could say we're speechless. But I did want to say thank you, from us. We're very fortunate that she is remembered always. It's a privilege that few people get to experience when they've lost someone in their lives. They don't always have them in front of them with recordings or photographs, or people's memories. Or occasions fifty years later, where people gather to pay tribute. But that is a blessing that we were given. As a child of four, I sometimes don't have a whole lot to contribute to the conversation. But having lived around the family, and being here in Winchester, with all her friends, the people who knew her, worked with her, and watched her grow, it has been a learning experience, a history lesson. My dad would've loved to have been here today. He still comes to Winchester and still loves to come, but he's gotten it down to just an occasional thing now. But he did want to send his best, and say thank you."

Jim also spoke that day, after walking slowly from his seat in the front row. He too opened with an unnecessary caveat that he didn't write a speech. "That day fifty years ago, that was the saddest day of my life." Overwhelmed, he simply listed memories, seriatim, with little commentary. He spoke about meeting Patsy for the first time, the WINC performance, the shows that followed. He mentioned his memorial parties for her, his respect for her talent. Heavy-heartedness fit him as unnaturally as his suit and tie. This was not a man made for tearful church services, but he muddled his way through, ending as he started: "That day was just so sad." Then he slowly returned to his seat next to Bertha.

Two doors by the podium swung open and we walked single file into the blinding funerary sun. The grave was right by the parking lot.

It was a modest thing, just a 3-foot metal marker on a marble base, flush with the ground at the outset of the cemetery. It was marked "DICK," and a large bouquet of roses, sent by Charlie, was sitting on the place where he was headed. The ground was still soft from a snowstorm earlier in the week, but the sun was out and a powerful wind tossed the men's ties and jackets as we stood in a circle around the plot, squinting and readjusting our feet.

One more emotional speaker read a final prayer. This was Jim Mogavoy, whose father drove Patsy's car in two Apple Blossom Parades in the late 1950s. He was born the same year as Patsy but stood tall and oaklike in his tartan jacket. "Her memory, fifty years later, is still alive for us," Mogavoy read from a piece of wind-shaken paper.

As the group began to break up, some attendees took pictures of the grave. Others approached Julie, who signed programs and stood for photos while the wind scrambled her black hair. But most people congregated in small groups for prolonged hugs. The wind kept toppling the graveside flowers, and David and the other docents sprinted over to stand them back up. At the perimeter, the blonde Channel 3 anchor stood in front of the camera recording her segment intro. Before long she had the microphone in front of JudySue, who spoke with a hushed, grateful nod: "Everything I'd hoped," she said. "Just . . . so perfect."

I stood in the blasting wind watching everyone come to terms with this difficult walk through the past, when out of the distance on the far side of the cemetery emerged a roving figure in a pink T-shirt. She came crookedly toward us as another woman in earth tones jogged to keep up with her. At close range she looked older than her manic walk implied, and unwell—rabid, possessed, overdetermined.

"What's all this?" she asked loudly. David approached, in shepherd-the-people mode, and explained our purpose for the day. The woman's eyes widened and her mouth fell open.

"I . . . I can't believe . . . Are you hearing him?" she asked her friend, who seemed equally shocked. She turned back to David. "I didn't even know Patsy Cline was from here. I didn't know . . ." She stopped to get her breath. "I love her. I live for her. A few days ago I told her," pointing to the friend, "I told her we had to get in the van and drive somewhere. I needed a break from everything. We just hit the road. I'm from Florida. We just ended up here."

No one knew what to make of her, and after trying without success to bring her into our mournful circle, even David left her to be. The news team knew a story when they saw one, however, and soon this woman was in front of the Channel 3 camera, breathlessly baring her desperate soul for the local audience that, in person, kept their safe distance, protecting the solemnity of their communal memory.

3

Resistance

Seventy-odd years earlier, back when Jim McCoy was just beginning to envision a world beyond rain, soil, and sun, the Valley land around Shenandoah Memorial Park contained some of the most active agricultural farms on earth. This was the peak of Virginia apple growing, the industry that literally brought light to the Shenandoah. At their height, Valley growers supplied two-thirds of the entire national apple supply, and the magnitude of picking, planting, and storing all that fruit required the region's first large-scale electrical grid. For that innovation, and for the scope and scale of Valley produce operations altogether, the locals owed a single man, Harry Flood Byrd. There can be no understanding of the Winchester region's particular character or twentieth-century evolution without Byrd. No one else had such an outsized effect on the upper Valley's physical and political state, or arguably the psychology of its residents. Byrd essentially created the world that allowed Jim McCoy to dream of a modern life, and he embodied the culture that pushed those dreams to the margins.

Born in 1887, Byrd knew all about the southern propensity for somber remembrance that Patsy's mourners exhibited around her grave site. He grew up in the era when Virginians, like their compatriots throughout the battered Confederacy, elevated communal mourning to an entire way of being. "The well-born Virginian of our era was tutored to revere himself as being the dispossessed heir to an all-perfect and all-admirable estate in the Old South," wrote the Richmond native James Branch Cabell, a popular author who was less than a decade older than Byrd. "We were taught that we had been robbed; that our rights had been taken away from us at Appomattox." Annual Confederate Memorial Day celebrations echoed throughout late-nineteenth-century Dixie, and reverence for Virginian Robert E. Lee approached deification, particularly in his home state. By his own admission, Byrd rarely read anything but Civil War histories throughout his life, and he surely would have known well Thomas Buchanan Read's popular postwar poem "Sheridan's Ride," commemorating the Union general's 1864 burning of the Valley—a poem that starts, "Up from the South at break of day/ Bringing to Winchester fresh dismay."

But despite his immersion in the cult of southern victimization, Byrd never evinced much passion for collective culture or experience. Byrd was born into one of Virginia's First Families, who trace their lines back to the colony's earliest blue-blooded English dynasties. Byrd's most famous ancestor was William Byrd II, the so-called Pepys of the Old Dominion, who was born in England in 1674 but lived most of his adult life in America as a legendary bon vivant, author, diarist, explorer-surveyor, and statesmen. William II served in the Virginia House of Burgesses and founded Richmond, naming it for an area of London that he knew from his years as a barrister. A long line of legally minded Byrds followed in his wake, though after the suicide of his son, William III, the family fell on lean times that lasted through the nineteenth century.

Harry's father, Richard Evelyn Byrd, came to Winchester for a fresh start on his own legal practice, and his sons rescued the family name. Richard Evelyn Byrd Jr. became a pioneering Antarctic explorer and the first man to fly across the southernmost continent. Harry, the older brother, barely left the Valley except for business, and looked, even in his earliest photos, like he was born with a starched collar and double Windsor knot. With his father, who favored him, Harry took regular trips to the family cabin near Appomattox, dubbed "the Byrd's Nest." There he developed a lifelong love for long forest walks, and a yen for solitude and meditative quiet. The young Harry surely needed those relaxing spells; his father was such a hapless and unreliable alcoholic that he once left a trial during recess and returned to court so drunk that he began arguing for the other side. Harry clearly took the behavior as a warning, and was a teetotaler all his life. He also exhibited a shocking work ethic from childhood, a hearty reserve of what Henry Adams called "the Virginian habit of command." Even relative to the brush-clearing Spotswood gang or Jim McCoy's ceaseless roaming pursuit of a country music career, no one ever attacked the Valley with such terrific force of will.

At age fifteen, Harry Byrd dropped out of high school and took over the *Winchester Star*, his father's failing newspaper. Guided by his stated editorial philosophy that "the Business Department is the life blood of the paper," he made it solvent within five years, then bought out his sole competitor. Byrd quickly ran with the highest class of corporate Virginia men, who drafted him to become a state senator.

By this time, Byrd had already begun growing apples on his land in Berryville, JudySue's hometown. This kind of amateur farming was so common in the region that it might as well have been a native folk tradition, as the McCoys' cider press attested. But apples themselves were originally a product of the British Empire. Pre-colonial Virginia was naturally rich with cherry, mulberry, gooseberry, and huckleberry, but apples arrived on the earliest English ships. They were abundant at Jamestown, where John Smith noted their use for "most excellent and comfortable drinks." By 1686, one Sir William Fitzhugh had 2,500 acres of apple trees in Westmoreland County, near the mouth of the Potomac, and many other men had smaller orchards for private use as well. William Byrd II even praised the state's "industrious" apple planters in his famous *History of the Dividing Line betwixt Virginia and North Carolina*, published in 1728. From the moment that Englishmen first saw the Valley from the Swift Run Gap, apples spread through the Shenandoah as quickly as the people. Before they became the quintessentially American fruit, apples were a living symbol of possibility, proof that British life and tastes could be imposed upon the New World.

Byrd didn't especially need the money, so his own initial growing efforts might be called a labor of love. But Harry Flood Byrd never did anything for sentimental reasons. He treated his trees like a hobby empire, a lower-stakes version of the political and media fiefdom he was growing with the *Star* and in the state house. He looked at the Shenandoah Valley of his youth—a quiet, comfortable place that was better known commercially for wheat—and saw a potential factory. Byrd bought his first apple land in 1906. In 1912, he expanded by purchasing his neighbor, Rosemont Orchard. In 1918, he bought nearby Green Orchard, then the next year, Kelly Orchard. His expansion was equaled only by his innovation. He brought heaters into his fields to protect the trees against spring freezes. He was the first planter in the area to use tractors. He pioneered the use of corrugated pads to keep his fruit unbruised. He volunteered his trees for some of the earliest large-scale pesticide and fertilizer tests.

As a businessman, Byrd was a visionary. As a politician, he was a great businessman. Winchester Cold Storage Company, which he built in 1917, wasn't the first such facility in Virginia, but it soon became the largest in the world. Despite his career-defining aversion to government debt, the project was financed with borrowed money; in 1920, Byrd owed over $150,000 to creditors, even as he became the stubborn face of "pay as you go" government budgeting. But he achieved the kind of success and influence that make mere hypocrisy irrelevant. World War I started just days after he opened the storage facility, for example, and threatened to doom it right at the start. So Byrd contacted a congressman friend to volunteer the facility as a place to store food for the war effort. Even as the fight in Europe waged on, Harry Byrd kept the trains coming into Winchester.

In the state senate, Byrd was a ceaseless advocate of limited government except when big government benefited him. He increased the power of the Crop Pest Commission, raising the standards of inspections beyond what smaller, competing operations could afford. He passed laws requiring cedar trees to be kept away from orchards to prevent infection from a type of mold called cedar rust, then had his neighbors' trees destroyed during the night if they didn't comply. He improved Winchester's surrounding highways, brush-cut non-apple trees from roadsides, and pushed for an extension of electric lines to supply the cold storage plant with better power. But he resisted any regulation of cold storage plants, as well as any size limits on trucks.

Despite his ruthlessness, Byrd was esteemed, and even relatable for local folks. His expressionless workaholism endeared him to a state that has produced more presidents than world-famous artists. He never lost his capacity for piddlin'. Like an upper-crust cousin to Jim McCoy, he tended to the minutest details of his business operations: poisoning mice, pruning trees for better sunlight, sales. "Ranging across his fields on foot, horseback, and motorcycle," writes one biographer, "he involved himself in every phase of the operation from purchasing land to planting trees—whose quality he was very particular about—to harvesting and selling the fruit." He was elected president of the Frederick County Fruit Growers association in 1920, and held an annual apple-growers picnic at Rosemont Orchard that attracted 1,500 guests at its apex.

In 1924, Byrd helped conceive the first Shenandoah Apple Blossom Festival, with a goal "to bring visitors from far and wide to Winchester and Frederick County that they might see the grandeur of our land at the time of its greatest beauty—apple blossom time." It started as a one-day, one-time event, but the chamber of commerce knew a gold-laying goose when they saw it. With a few wartime exceptions, the festival has come annually ever since, and now stretches over a week and a half in late April, as my tipsy brunette friend had informed me in the Half Note Lounge. And it all started when Harry Byrd—the man who built more roads and power lines and cut down more trees throughout the Valley than anyone in history—sold the idea on "the grandeur of our land."

His rise became inexorable, self-fulfilling. In 1926, Byrd became governor, the youngest since Jefferson, and his youthful-
ness was a major part of his appeal: "The vigor with which he
moved generated a wave of optimism and acclaim," according to
one historian. He was additionally the bringer of a new techno-
logical dawn, the first head of Virginia to use a microphone and
speakers at his inauguration and the first to broadcast the ceremony on the radio. His speech nevertheless announced that "the
prosperity of Virginia depends primarily upon agriculture."

By 1933, Byrd's orchards were producing half a million bushels from 150,000 trees. The Winchester Cold Storage Company
held 1.5 million bushels at any given time, and Byrd began selling
overseas, to England especially. Byrd's net worth at this time was
$1 million. Apples may have epitomized early Shenandoah Eng-
lishness, but Byrd, by using them as an instrument of personal
fortune and political domination, ushered in the region's era of
unfettered American business. He took a symbol of his people's
settlement and turned it into a monopoly.

In March of that year, the undisputed "Apple King of America" was appointed to the United States Senate after his prede-
cessor was drafted into the Roosevelt administration. The me-
dian income in the South during the Depression was half that
in the North, which led President Roosevelt to famously declare
the South "the nation's No. 1 economic problem." His stimulus
plans included massive efforts to modernize the region, usually
through the Works Progress and Public Works administrations.
In almost all cases, Byrd, an arch-Dixiecrat, opposed these mea-
sures in alliance with his fellow Virginian newspaperman-sena-
tor Carter Glass, from Lynchburg. But even as the two bemoaned
federal overreach and overspending with their every breath, between 1935 and 1943, Virginia, like the South generally, gained

huge amounts of new roads and electric lines, and significantly lowered its infant mortality rate, among other public health improvements. As the Depression and recovery wore on, Byrd had his apple pie and ate it too: the New Deal strengthened his constituents and his home infrastructure, while his virulent opposition to it made him a folk hero in a state that honored noble self-sufficiency above all. As his own agricultural fortunes soared, he voted against numerous farm bills and worked hard to undermine the Civil Works Administration, a short-lived manual-labor employment program. He borrowed hundreds of thousands of dollars at a time to improve his own business while lecturing the peons about the impossibility of free lunch. When an Alexandria school principal asked to pick postharvest apples in order to feed students, Byrd told him to go to the shops in Winchester and buy them through the proper channels like everyone else.

The postwar New South boom compelled white people from the country to move toward the city—even Jim McCoy went briefly to Baltimore in the late 1940s to work for Bethlehem Steel. Byrd was always good for a speech about the value of rural work, but his decades of greatest influence corresponded with the era of disappearing farmers. He was now the paterfamilias of the so-called Byrd Machine, a political king-making operation that rivaled New York's Tammany Hall in terms of overall influence over an entire state. No political decision in Virginia could be made without the participation and profit of Byrd's network, and that was certainly true of immigration reform. Migrants from Mexico came in to replace the lost white workers, and Byrd brought them onto his orchards without question. In the late 1950s, he employed 1,800 men, women, and children picking his fruit from 200,000 trees. He had eleven orchards over 5,000 acres, plus five packinghouses, one cannery, three cold storage units, five camp houses, sixty 2-ton trucks, fifty-three high-pressure sprayers, 400,000 picking boxes, and 25,000 smudge pots. He opened a cannery to process lower-quality fruit into jelly, butter, and cider. He worked in the Senate to limit regulation on migrant labor, while opposing legislation that required that Mexican workers earn 90 percent of a state's average farm wages.

Byrd's end-of-year personal financial statement for 1963, the same year his newspaper compared Patsy Cline's mourners to crazed bargain-bin shoppers, listed physical assets at $4.5 million and an equal amount in stocks. His apple business alone was worth $1.5 million. He gave more than $50,000 to charity. This unstoppable worker and builder had nothing left to push against, and only a dwindling claim to his long-held self-definition as a humble Valley farmer. As if in recognition of this, Harry Flood Byrd mounted one final obsessive campaign on behalf of his people, the vanishing white rural conservative class.

Virginia was spared the worst horrors and tensions of the civil rights movement. There were no commonwealth equivalents to the march on Selma, the brutal dog-and-firehose crackdowns in Montgomery, or the assassination of Martin Luther King Jr. The Ku Klux Klan was kept largely at bay thanks to antilynching legislation passed by Byrd himself as governor. But in 1959, at the peak of Harry Flood Byrd's political and commercial control, the state experienced its worst episode of overt reactionary cruelty: Prince Edward County, down toward the North Carolina line that William Byrd II helped draw, decided it would rather close all of its public schools rather than accommodate desegregation. For five years, white families pulled together a makeshift private school operation that, by design, their black neighbors couldn't afford. More than a thousand black children missed five years of formal education. For once, Virginians looked like plain old backwoods bigots: the county government even warned that integration would make "the people of America a mongrel nation." Attorney General Robert Kennedy decried Prince Edward County's actions as "a disgrace to our country," while *Time* magazine called the school closings "the most infamous segregationist tactic in the U.S."

Byrd saw it differently. To his mind, "the gallant little county of Prince Edward is fighting against great odds to protect a principle it believes to be right." When the Supreme Court ordered the district to desegregate, he called the ruling "tyrannical," just as, in the original wake of *Brown v. Board,* he joined with Strom Thurmond to write and distribute the so-called Southern Manifesto that decried the ruling as an "abuse of judicial power." In 1958, Byrd claimed that racial equality was the South's "gravest crisis since the War Between the States." Byrd put a name to the proud effort to stop desegregation at all costs: massive resistance. In a speech on the Senate floor, he compelled all the "southern states" to join Virginia in collective opposition.

The effort was no match for the well-organized, morally upright movement for black equality. By the time that Prince Edward County was finally forced to enroll black students in 1964, this racist campaign had tarnished Byrd's reputation as a benevolent businessman-king. Massive resistance was controversial even in his own party and his own state. Byrd's sole Virginia partners were the so-called Southside Seven, a collection of deep-rural state senators who he met with in rooms with confederate flags unfurled on the walls. Together they proposed "compromises" that kept black kids out of public schools while rescinding the tax-exempt status of the NAACP. The blatant attack on civil rights put the decades-old Byrd Machine on the ropes at last. In 1960, the so-called Young Turks, a group of businessmen from the D.C. suburbs, ran a coordinated electoral campaign to undercut Byrd's plantation-bound view of the world and the races. They couldn't quite finish him off just then, but the man was getting old anyway. Byrd left office in 1965, and died of cancer in 1966.

Byrd's personal prosperity obscured the fact that he actually lost all the major battles he claimed to stand for. Black children entered Virginia schools. Debt still drove political spending. And even though he embodied the rural patrician class, his tenure as a lawmaker coincided with the end of that class and the entire culture surrounding it. He was the most powerful man in the South as it underwent the transition from agrarian to urban—from battery-powered farmhouse Victrolas to neon-bedecked honky-tonks. During the 1950s, as Byrd's wealth exploded thanks to limitless cheap Mexican labor and a stranglehold on all federal and state budgeting, southern cities expanded at thirteen times the rate of rural areas. By 1960, a majority of Virginians, including Jim McCoy and his young family, lived in cities and suburbs. With the growing urban population, the power center of Virginia shifted from Byrd country to the Washington beltway as soon as he was gone. By the end of the '60s, Democrats couldn't abide their southern senators' hideous racism, and they abandoned the South altogether.

Byrd's beloved fruit industry fared no better. In 1937, back when the Valley apple industry was the envy of the world and Byrd was basically a living god, there were nearly 4,000 apple growers managing 4 million trees in Virginia. But by 2005, there were barely 200 growers managing 1.5 million trees. Cold storage and global shipping, Byrd's biggest business triumphs, eventually became the Winchester industry's executioner; growers in Washington State and China are now just as capable of holding hundreds of thousands of bushels indefinitely. Those places also have more open land for the industry to slowly devour, and their climates are better suited to apple growing. Over five decades, Byrd built a Virginia that served him best, and when he died all his supposed values vanished with him.

Surely he sensed this. By the 1960s, Byrd was the de facto leader of the entire southern political establishment. He spoke for the whole region, not only Virginia, and I give him the benefit of the doubt to assume that he grasped, in his senescence, that his own astonishing success had done nothing to enrich the sainted land to which he claimed such allegiance. Having sold out the South for personal gain, trampling its communal culture while privatizing his section of its lush green hills, this creature of Confederate Memorial Days and "war of northern aggression" revisionism made one last-ditch effort on behalf of southern valor. In an eerie parallel, his doomed resistance campaign coincided, almost to the year, with the Civil War's centennial. In his own way, Byrd clung to past ideals as much as Patsy Cline's devoted fans. As the world around him grew more complicated and foreign-seeming, and as he grew more isolated from his own upbringing, Byrd grew more committed to familiar, triumphant attitudes. Massive resistance, like opening up a mountaintop country bar or refurbishing a legend's old house, was a way to feel strong again as the old order slipped away—with the obvious, tragic difference that Byrd had orchestrated the old order's demise himself, nearly single-handedly, over long, cruel decades.

Byrd's values, his way of life, his political will, and even his personal reputation were seemingly dead as dust by the time he retired. But no legend dies that easily in Winchester, where people still talk about George Washington like he just ran out to grab beer. When I first started visiting, it often felt like Byrd still ran the place. I would typically drive in on Route 7, the road connecting Winchester to Washington's suburbs, which was christened the Harry F. Byrd Highway in 1968. Passing through Berryville, where Rosemont Mansion still stands as a historic site and popular event venue, I entered the city just north of Shenandoah University's Harry F. Byrd, Jr. School of Business, named for his son, and drove past the offices of the *Winchester Star*, which remains Byrd-owned and nostalgically reactionary.

Downtown, I would park and walk along Piccadilly Street, where visitors are invited to pretend that apples still define the area. I'd stroll past the massive, gleaming fiberglass apple adorned with painted portraits of notable Winchesterites, including Richard Evelyn Byrd Jr., depicted in a heavily ruffed Arctic coat. Around the corner, near the George Washington Hotel, I'd see the little red offices of the Apple Blossom Festival, and then right before coming to the eastern end of the commercial district, the small headquarters of Glaize Apples, LLC, one of the last remaining dynasties of the Shenandoah produce boom. The Glaize family still operates a genuine growing orchard about 15 miles outside town; they haven't sold all the land to developers, haven't adopted the cost-effective but regulation-burdened model of mashing subpar fruit into sauce or juice or baby food, and haven't sold the organization to an out-of-state behemoth. (The physical components of the famed Byrd operation now belong to White House Foods, which operates the huge red-brick factories and cold storage units near the stone wall that Jim Mc-

Coy's guitar teacher, Pete Kelly, built.) But the Glaizes have diversified—into real estate, mostly, though also into corporate
statesmanship. Because of their proximity to Washington, Phil
Glaize Jr., the grandson of the company's founding grower, lob-
bied Congress for years on behalf of the United States Apple
Association.

I have walked through the Glaizes' geometric tree rows, ad-
miring the misty, gnarled beauty of an old-fashioned orchard
during the late-autumn harvest season. I have eaten their fruit
straight from the tree and had to close my eyes in ecstasy as
I chewed. It tasted like pure cold sunlight and tart honey, and
made me regret whatever fridge-bound Styrofoam I'd lately accepted as an apple. This privilege still exists in Winchester. The
farmers' markets abound with fruit and vegetables that make
country life seem like the only sensible human pursuit. But it's
not getting any easier to grow the stuff or make a living off it.
The smaller farmers wake hours before dawn to drive their product to markets in Maryland or Pennsylvania, while Glaize Apples, an operation that once rivaled Byrd's for sheer market vis-
ibility, sells a majority of its fruit to Walmart.

One Sunday morning I was walking through Piccadilly Street
in search of a meal that, for now, you still can't find in any big-box
store: an all-American breakfast. Even in these globalized times,
every respectable Main Street in the country has at least one
Formica-filled haven that serves coffee, pig meat, eggs, and toast
until 2 p.m., and yet no such place appeared in downtown Winchester. Alone, I walked past storefront after storefront, want-
ing only a padded swivel stool and a laminated menu. Finally I
arrived at the glass window that had once drawn JudySue's ire,
the place with the spray-painted name, JUST LIKE GRANDMA'S,

and would have kept walking if I hadn't glimpsed two figures moving at the far end of the counter. A small diner. The heart sings.

Inside, a young black man was cleaning his kitchen while an older black woman watched. Slowly, drowsily, he collected his stainless steel bowls and wiped down the hood of his grill. The woman, his only customer so far, sat at the counter eating a simple egg sandwich and talking about their mutual friends. I took a seat at the opposite end of the counter to grant them their privacy, between the window and a small radio mounted on a wall shelf. A contemporary gospel station played as the young man, dreadlocks tumbling out through the back of his bandana, came over with a menu, a mug, and a coffee pot.

"Take your time," he said, turning back to his housekeeping. I took a small sip of my scalding, perfectly brewed coffee and consulted the offerings. The glory of an all-American breakfast is its balance of extremes: salty and sweet, formulaic and customizable, as plain as Shaker furniture but as indulgent as a birthday cake. It's only eggs, meat, and carbohydrates, none of which require special culinary skill, but this is America damn it, so you —the strong-willed, self-made breakfast eater—are implored to assert yourself. What kind of meat? What manner of eggs? White or wheat toast?

When the cook returned I ordered the same combo I always do: eggs over easy, bacon, wheat toast. I added two pancakes to compound the hedonism. Then I gently tossed the menu on the counter with satisfaction.

As my host turned back to the grill and began assembling his tools for the job, I looked up at the wall, where a framed article from the *Winchester Star* hung just below the stereo speaker. It was a scissored-out clip from the Food section, page C5, dated September 26, 2012.

CAFE MIXES THE OLD THE NEW

WINCHESTER — Perry Davis likes getting different opinions before he puts new items on the menu at Just Like Grandma's Cafe and Carryout in Winchester.

Customers are frequent taste-testers, and Davis values their input. But whenever possible, Davis likes getting the opinion of someone he knows will tell the truth — his great-grandmother, Viola Lampkin Brown, 100, of Berryville.
"She will definitely tell me what she thinks and if something's missing or needs to be changed," Davis, 29, of Winchester, said.

Brown's picture and another great-grandmother of Davis', the late Betty Killam-Rogers, sit on a shelf overlooking the small kitchen and 15-seat counter that take up most of the diner at 46 E. Piccadilly St. The photos are a tribute to the two biggest culinary influences in Davis' life and a constant reminder of what he is trying to achieve with his restaurant, which opened July 27.

I read that Perry inherited a meat-and-potatoes menu from the Piccadilly Grill, a twenty-year-old institution that had held the property until its owner's death. The rest of the article included a list of the dishes that Perry had slowly incorporated into the repertoire: fried catfish (imported from Louisiana), curry chicken salad, a frittata, baked tilapia topped with crabmeat. He spoke about using real vanilla bean in his French toast, turmeric in the chicken, mace in the baked goods, and mango and pine nuts in a specialty salad. He was incorporating his relatives' personal recipes as well, including meat loaf, pound cake, and lemon meringue pie. He'd also spent some years in the kitchen of the Dancing Goat, the luxury restaurant on the first floor of the George Washington Hotel across the street.

At the center of the newspaper story was a picture of Perry with his surviving great-grandmother, the woman who taught him how to cook. They both looked focused and proud. And why not: watching him begin his work, I considered how rare it was to see a black-owned business in town. Discussions of race in Winchester tend to focus on Latinos, since immigration from Mexico and Central America has been the leading source of demographic change since at least the 1980s. The bulk of Philip Glaize Jr.'s congressional testimony involves immigration reform, which he favors, since his entire apple-picking workforce is foreign-born. But black and white issues are trickier, subtler, in keeping with the grand Virginia tradition of simmering racial tensions rather than explosive ones.

Perry clicked the burners on and reached under his counter to pop open the fridge doors. He pulled out a few eggs and a tub of butter, from which he spooned out a golf-ball-size chunk and placed on the shining silver grill top. It instantly bubbled and slid as he commenced a batter in a steel bowl. Flour, soda, a small pinch of salt, white sugar—they all entered the bowl in quick, economical motions, unmeasured but precise. Then he cracked in a couple eggs and reached back into the fridge for a carton of buttermilk. He stirred with an old wire whisk, not too fast but steady, until the batter seemed to almost move on its own. Then he reached back into the fridge and pulled out a package of thick-cut bacon, pulled out four slices, and laid them down like newborns on the buttered, rumbling range. They popped and puckered and the room smelled like fat and smoke. Then he grabbed a small ladle and added three dots of pancake bat-

ter to the glistening surface, spreading them out with the uten-
sil's bottom until they achieved perfect roundness. Then he set
everything down, grabbed the coffee pot, and walked over to fill
my mug back up.

I could have paid then and there. It was a pleasure to watch
him work. The woman at the other end of the counter sat there
bending his ear the entire time. She was missing at least two
teeth, and from her conversation—about friends, wrongdoings,
old memories—I gleaned that she was a lot younger than she
looked. Perry had little to say, but he laughed with her, smiled,
and agreed with every characterization as she told every story.
She clearly needed to talk, needed to speak out loud and add to
the atmosphere. As Jim said, some folks need to get it out.

Perry gave everything one flip with a spatula, then pulled out
a platter and put two slices of wheat bread in the toaster. When
the pancakes rose, he swept the whole meal off the range top
with a few balletic gestures and delivered an absolutely photo-
worthy plate to me, topping up the coffee and handing over cutlery and a few napkins. I took the syrup and smothered everything, then picked up a forkful of pancakes with a bit of bacon
speared at the end, lifted it to my mouth, and if there hadn't
been a hallelujah chorus playing on the radio I would have heard
one anyway. Those classic all-American extremes were balanced perfectly. The cakes were clouds, the bacon was a braid of
half-melted fat and crisp streaks. I split the yolk of the eggs and
watched the yellow-orange ooze out like molasses. The toast—
which, like everything else, was nearly translucent with butter—
absorbed it hungrily.

From the catfish to the plentiful butter, Perry's cooking was
straight from the down-home country cookbook. Only lard or
grits would have made it more so. But the all-American is unique

for being essentially region-less. You can find it anywhere, almost never with local additions. In Kennebunkport or Scottsdale, bacon and eggs are bacon and eggs, and accordingly, it is highway food. Drive any interstate and you will pass billboard after billboard with two shining yolks and a couple strips on a nondescript plate. It is a primary lure of Cracker Barrels, fast-food franchises, and discount hotel chains. It belies no ethnicity or foreign influence. It is simply American, like big-finned Buicks, the Stratocaster, jukeboxes, or Marilyn Monroe. Or Patsy Cline.

His paid work momentarily done, Perry turned back to his stovetop and set a double boiler over heat. He cracked a few more eggs and skillfully juggled them back and forth to separate the yolks, which he threw in the bowl and whisked, nodding along with his friend's latest tale. After a minute Perry added a little butter, still whisking, then a little more, whisking faster still. Then he cracked a couple eggs into his second pot and split an English muffin. He reached back in the fridge and tossed a slice of thick ham onto the grill next to them, then resumed his stirring. When he pulled out the whisk it carried a cup of lush gold sauce in its wires, and he watched—his weary eyes staring intently, like a hypnotist's—as the dense, bright treasure curled and drizzled back into its bowl.

"Made something for you," he told his friend, who had finished her sandwich and sat quietly at last, staring up at the lazily tilting fan on the ceiling. He put the toasted muffin halves on a plate, pulled the ham off the grill with tongs, then scooped the poached eggs from their pot and laid them on gently. He sliced a lemon and squeezed its juice into his sauce, added salt and pepper, then ladled a ribbon onto the eggs.

"That's called eggs Benedict," he told her. She looked toward the plate with distrust. Perry laughed.

"Come on now," he said. "You have to try it. Tell me if I should put it on the menu."

"What's that yellow?" She poked it with a fork. The choir proclaimed Jesus's glory.

"Hollandaise sauce," he told her. "That's real food."

"I never eaten no holiday sauce," she said, which made Perry double over with laughter.

"*Hollandaise,* with an S at the end. Ain't nothing called holiday sauce." Cautiously, the woman cut a piece and took a bite. She looked even more skeptical once she chewed.

"It's good," she said. "I don't wanna eat anymore but it's good." Perry could barely contain himself. At last another customer came, another lone white guy with a crew cut and his plaid shirt tucked into his jeans. He looked his menu over while the fan turned, the gospel soared, the grill hummed, the coffee burbled, and a hard-living woman ate her first-ever eggs Benedict. I swirled a piece of pancake in a pond of butter, syrup, and yolk. Perry came over to fill my coffee; it had never even gotten half-empty since I'd been there.

"Gotta teach these people about real food," he said under his breath, and I wasn't sure if my own gluttonous breakfast was being indicted. But I sat there, under Viola Lampkin Brown's century-old gaze, across the street from a giant fiberglass apple, and thought to myself: Greater obstacles have been overcome.

PART TWO

NEW WAYS

4

A Museum and a Mountaintop

THE MUSEUM OF THE SHENANDOAH Valley isn't typically open at 9 a.m. on Saturday mornings, but this was a special occasion: Labor Day weekend, eight days before what would have been Patsy Cline's eighty-first birthday. And most important, it was the morning of the grand-opening party for the museum's newest exhibit, *Becoming Patsy Cline*, a years-in-the-making collaboration between the curators and JudySue Huyett-Kempf's organization, Celebrating Patsy Cline. In the wide beaming light of the floor-length conference-room windows, JudySue and her people ambled in and made for the circular, skirted table. They got their plates and hovered around the loose pyramids of scones and Danishes, passing tongs by the spiraling napkin towers.

The men and women near this mountain of flaky carbs and

drizzled icing were members of the Always Patsy Cline Fan Organization, and had been invited for a private preview of the exhibit before a country-themed gala that night. Established in 1987, the APCFO is the only official Patsy fan club, charging $15 annual dues ($25 for couples) that entitle members to special offers on merchandise, a quarterly zine, and an invitation to the annual Labor Day gathering in Winchester. For many years, Charlie Dick, Patsy's widower and her legacy's faithful steward, ran the organization and hosted the fall festivities, though the leadership had fallen out of the family until recently, when Julie decided to take the helm. Of course, for decades Winchester wasn't much of a destination except for the ambience; the only Patsy site was her headstone, though the true pilgrims could always head to the Troubadour for Jim's annual Sunday picnic, a tradition since 1964. But now, in 2013, the historic Cline House was a going tourist concern, Celebrating Patsy Cline appeared ascendant, and the museum had prepared and heavily publicized this exhibit—the first since its opening in 2005 to stray from the unquestioned Wealth, Washington, and War template of Valley greatness.

Around the breakfast buffet, the main conversation concerned who was feeling ambitious enough to get up to the Troubadour in the evening and on Sunday. Julie corroborated that Jim and Bertha had been busy all week preparing for their capstone summer party. Other than two women in their early thirties— a lawyer and a social worker from Washington, D.C.—I was the youngest person around the pastry tower by a good twenty-five years. A few were elderly or near it, the men in camel-hair jackets and their wives in pantsuits and pearls. You could see them weighing the forty-five-minute drive against a strictly regimented bedtime and meal schedule. But everyone agreed that the Troubadour was a worthy destination, this weekend most of all, and some had even been to the picnic before. They spoke of seeing the six-shooter smoker like it was the Elgin Marbles.

Julie arrived with her husband, Richard, a working-class Nashville native just like her. If you didn't know that she was Patsy's daughter, her high-cheeked smile would have given it away, though the waist-length, LP-black hair cascading around her shoulders testified to her long-standing taste for '70s rock over country. She greeted everyone warmly as they loaded up on breakfast and found seats at the conference tables around the carpeted room, then ceded the floor to Julie Armel, the museum's director of marketing.

"Welcome, and what an honor to have the official Patsy fan club here to open this event," said Armel, who was also a good bit younger than the average attendee, though she wore pearls of her own and a bright pink jacket—the very model of a public liaison for a heavily endowed private historical museum. "This has been such a long time coming, and I know it means so much for us to have you all here, especially Julie, to open this unique exhibition."

Her white-haired audience had their backs to the windows, through which the museum grounds were glowing in hazy late-summer light befitting their grand origins. Though the building we were sitting in had been raised less than a decade earlier, the surrounding land was some of the most hallowed in the Shenandoah. It was here that the English surveyor James Wood settled with his wife in the early eighteenth century, and it was he who donated land to the state of Virginia in 1744 for the establishment of Winchester, née Frederick Town. Wood's own estate stayed a family property, and his son built the famed Glen Burnie mansion, one of the most opulent in post-Revolutionary Virginia, in

1794. In the nineteenth century, Wood's grandson married into the Glass family, members of which eventually left Virginia for Oklahoma where they made a fortune in the oil business. The mansion and its six surrounding acres simply sat there, a massive family retreat on the west end of the city, as Winchester's downtown grew and the surrounding section of Frederick County became famous for wheat, then apples.

In 1959, as Harry Byrd was running out of worlds to conquer and Patsy Cline was escaping his clutches for Nashville, an Oklahoma-born descendant named Julian Wood Glass Jr. compelled his boyfriend, R. Lee Taylor, to return to Glen Burnie and restore it to its initial glory. Glass was a renowned art collector and aesthete, and he and Taylor saw the Wood family property as a grand canvas in brick, plaster, and soil. As greater Winchester fell into a midcentury frenzy of modernization—interstates, outside businesses, immigration—this man with the founder's name gave new life to its oldest manse, reclaiming it as a palace of stunning landscaping, matchless interior design, and regal entertaining for the blue bloods and their set. He returned the gardens to their former glory, installing fountains, stone sculptures, pillars, and a cocktail pavilion. The home itself, meanwhile, became the venue for Glass and Taylor's renowned collection of eighteenth- and nineteenth-century art, instruments, and decorative domestic pieces, especially Taylor's fourteen antique dollhouses.

Despite the earth-shaking physical and cultural changes taking place, this was still the era when Winchester's purportedly gay children were treated with conversion therapies and sodomy laws were in place and enforced. It almost goes without saying that Glass and Taylor were not "out" by any contemporary measure. In their papers, which have been saved at the museum, they used the code "1-2-3" to communicate "I love you," though it must have been an open secret to their rarified strata of visitors that these two unmarried, cohabitating art-and-dollhouse collectors weren't merely roommates, companions, or any other decorous euphemism. Glass was not a public figure like his ancestor; he sought no formal office or influence, and lived only to reestablish his family's ties to history. In midcentury Winchester, money allowed him the incomplete freedom to live in the closet, compromised yet unharmed. His relationship was simultaneously privileged and constrained, and as complex as such an arrangement might require: Taylor and Glass actually broke up in the 1970s, though Taylor remained on the property in a guesthouse. United in genuine affinity for each other and the historic property they remade, they kept working on the house together into their old age, and planning for it to outlast them. By the time both men died in the 1990s, they had arranged for the mansion to become part of a larger historical complex, and the Museum of the Shenandoah Valley opened a decade later, with a mixture of old money and newer corporate masters on its board and funders' list.

This conference room, in other words, was the final iteration of a three-centuries-old fortune, the sort that once could shield even gay men from scorn. It would have been unimaginable for a resident of South Kent Street to have ever made it here as a visitor during Patsy's lifetime, when Glen Burnie was essentially the Versailles of the Valley and the *Star* still wouldn't give her the front page for Carnegie Hall. Now she was the subject of a well-publicized, curated homage. If ever proof were needed that the old battle lines were shifting in this community, here it was. If an expensive, expansive cultural institution was to survive here in the twenty-first century, it would need to tempt the region's middle class, many of whom were more interested and invested in Patsy's story than in an oil scion's vase collection.

"So who's ready to see Becoming Patsy Cline?" asked Julie Armel, whose name rang a bell. I flipped through old notes while our aging crowd raised themselves out of the chairs and a few husbands returned to the pastry table to grab a couple for the road. Down a sunlit hallway we went, through the museum lobby and into a wide doorless entryway that opened to a brightly lit map of the Valley stretching up to the ceiling. Titled "Virginia's Virginia," the map was overlaid with a dotted-line trail snaking through every little burg that Patsy had ever spent time in, from her childhood up through her singing career: Middletown, Elkton, Edinburg, Round Hill, and especially Lexington. A small sign acknowledged the exhibit's underwriters: Celebrating Patsy Cline, of course, as well as the Winchester Harley-Davidson dealership, Shenandoah Country Q102, and the state of Virginia—still, as ever, for lovers.

We walked in, Julie leading the charge. The fan club made a mockery of the museum's no-photography rule. They snapped away at the life-size archival photographs spread across the wall and at the many artifacts on display to tell the story of Virginia Hensley's transformation. There was Hilda's sewing machine and a few of the dresses she made for her daughter; the porch glider that sat outside the South Kent Street front door; and the original microphone from WINC, the one that Jim stood and sang behind on Saturday mornings. It was a massive metal contraption, more weapon than broadcasting instrument, like the hood ornament of a quadruple-size Cadillac.

One couple, middle-aged South Carolinians, found this item particularly satisfying. The woman posed as her husband, in Clemson baseball hat and matching windbreaker, took a photo.

"Carol Glass-Cooper," she introduced herself, hand out-stretched, once the picture was taken. "My husband Mark and I do a Patsy tribute. He plays Jim."

"'Daily Walkin' with Patsy,'" Mark chimed in, scrolling through his phone's photos.

"We're performing tonight at the Troubadour," Carol continued excitedly. "Jim invited us up. We've had him down in Seneca for one of our shows before. He sat right onstage with us."

Other than the microphone and this one excited couple, however, Jim's role was muted in the exhibit. Instead it was full of lushly written descriptions of Patsy's early days and little-seen images that showed just how many stylistic iterations she had gone through before her eventual emergence as an elegant Nashville chanteuse. One photograph showed her fronting a band in a sequined minidress and tall heels, while another caption described her brief stint as a singer for a big-band jazz outfit in the early 1950s. Elsewhere, the original *Star* story on her plane crash revealed just how small she seemed relative to the superstars onboard: "A silver belt buckle engraved with the name 'Hawkshaw Hawkins' was found near the wreckage. A woman's red slip was hanging from a tree."

The centerpiece, however, was a full room devoted to her performance on Arthur Godfrey's variety show. No video of the performance exists, but the audio had been discovered and cleaned up for this display. I sat down on one of the benches and listened to the whole clip, which lasted about ten minutes. Apparently Godfrey had read through his sponsor messages too quickly and had to kill time as Patsy and the house band prepared for the cameras. His tactic was to interview Hilda, who was in New York as Patsy's sponsor for the show, and he spent the greater part of their conversation discussing the ladies' homeland.

When she said she was from Winchester, Godfrey asked, "Are you a farmer?" Hilda said no, she was "a dressmaker and a homemaker."

She explained that she wasn't born in Winchester, but in a small town on North Mountain in the Blue Ridge. Godfrey had spent time in the area, on Catoctin Ridge near Frederick, Maryland. "It looked blue from a distance," he said, to the murmuring delight of his audience. "But then I've never seen a mountain range that didn't look blue from a distance. Not sure why they call it that."

He went on, rambling—you could almost hear him peering through the curtains to see when his band was ready. He knew that Winchester was "a big part of the war between the states," and that the area was "big apple country." That, and her current place on Decca Records, was all the mass television audience knew of Patsy Cline before she finally made her debut, preceded by a blast of horns that introduced a slower, sultrier version of "Walkin' After Midnight" than would appear on record a few weeks later, more of a blues than a country torch song. Patsy leaned into it. Her timing, as ever, was impeccable; she tugged at her low notes and sent the high ones heavenward. Godfrey was right to be impressed, and his audience screamed for her when it came time to choose the episode's ultimate winner. A few of the assembled fan club members sitting in the room with me applauded as well.

The message, both of Godfrey's interview and the museum that gave it pride of place in the story of Patsy's "becoming," was that she belonged to the Shenandoah Valley, to Virginia. She was apparently a product of apples and Civil War nostalgia and hills that rolled into western Maryland and beyond. I squirmed. Not because this assessment was necessarily wrong, but because it wasn't adequate. Patsy Cline didn't acquire firsthand experience of heartbreak and alienation from the Blue Ridge Mountains or Skyline Drive. She got those from Winchester specifically, from the people who treated her family and her music with unconcealed contempt. She got it from a rigid social hierarchy that wasn't unique to the town, but which certainly defined its residents' lives. That hierarchy forced her into an early marriage out of desperation, a marriage that strengthened her resolve to sing rather than submit to domesticity. It forged her connection to similar outsiders like Jim McCoy, and informed her worldwide fame as an icon of quiet, unflappable dignity in the face of despair. She wasn't Patsy Cline because of the Shenandoah—she was Patsy Cline because she grew up poor in its haughtiest city.

Our tour ended just as the museum opened for general visitors. I wandered into the permanent exhibits, which were spread throughout a low-lit, brown-hued room with re-creations of campsites, Indian ceremonies, and early European settlers' homesteads. This was a temple to noble landscapes and agricultural inheritance, an orderly linear progression from native farming to hardscrabble pioneer living.

But off to one side, a temporary exhibition leapt a century into the future. Moveable Feasts: Entertaining at Glen Burnie was a small but luxurious view into the splendor at Julian Wood Glass Jr.'s home in 1960. "Be our guest and travel with us to those halcyon days," beckoned a placard. "The family clock is chiming your arrival, just in time for brunch. So please, won't you come in? It is a fine day to visit the entertaining Glen Burnie."

The room's decadence made our gluttonous conference-room sugar feast seem almost monastic. Crystal champagne flutes were arranged next to pewter ice buckets, gilded plates, and serving platters. Julian's own dinner jacket and bejeweled cuff links stood proud on a wooden display near his cigarette case. A "Cocktails at the Pink Pavilion" case described Julian's effortless balance of eighteenth-century sophistication and Rat Pack cool. Through another doorway was a room of R. Lee Taylor's dollhouses, which were large enough for young children to stand comfortably inside the frames. The miniatures were outfitted and designed with the same exacting care and detail that marked Glass and Taylor's full-scale entertaining: upholstered chairs, chandeliers, sconces, little woven rugs. I'd never envied dolls before.

Yet the saving grace of all this gauche lavishness was the fact that it was designed for humans, not toys. There was something relatable in Glass and Taylor's eagerness to parade and entertain. However walled-off their life was, however inaccessible to the common person, it was endearing that they spent their fortune and good taste in service of their friends' enjoyment. At the exact moment that I was ogling their china table settings, Jim and Bertha were up on Highland Ridge preparing for their own annual blowout. It would be store-brand meat and weathered picnic furniture, not fountain-side champagne and caviar, but the basic purpose would be the same: communal luxury, a set-apart world of food and leisure, and yes, a little showmanship for its own sake. It was no secret why, in Winchester, I kept finding myself inside carefully recreated historic homes. From the moment that Englishmen came up and settled it, this area has always been up for grabs. Statesmen have claimed it as forcefully as singers, First Family nobility as well as mountain families. Winchester's residents have always been engaged in the process of defining this place and its character, and those definitions are often forged in living rooms more than state houses or courtrooms. That's where people learn their values and hear their legends. Homes—the places to gather with your people—were the true currency of a region in perpetual search of itself.

For the Boots, Beer, and BBQ event that evening, the museum had set up a huge tent outside, adjacent to the pleached allée and cocktail pavilion in the gardens. Hundreds of visitors were streaming in by 4 p.m. We entered and received our beer tickets and complementary plastic pint glass, which was emblazoned with the exhibit title and sponsors.

The crowd under that warm late-summer evening was even more uniform than the fan club. It was exclusively white, middle-aged couples in their casual finery, maneuvering through the tent with beers in each hand. The more flamboyant men wore ostentatious cowboy hats and armor-grade belt buckles, though most were content with untucked short-sleeve plaid button-downs. They followed their wives, who walked slowly in hoop earrings and long sleeveless blouses. Once they settled, they went back up to the food line, a long pulled-pork buffet. There was a band onstage by the gardens, a modern country group from North Carolina, and the meat, too, had a distinct vinegary Tar Heel taste. I grabbed my sandwich, asked for extra coleslaw and corn fritters, and sat in an empty picnic chair by the edge of the festivities.

The band had nothing to do with the kind of music that Patsy played. Like many country groups since the 1980s, they sounded more like a rock band than a honky-tonk one: everything was midtempo with the guitars up front and the drums loud and pounding, pedal steel floating above it all. The singer's voice was in the Waylon vein, a deep twang that stepped up higher for the songs about beer and lower for the ones about women, God, and daddy. He looked massive on the stage, with long stringy hair and a goatee like a grizzly's paw. The solos echoed through the tent as their audience discussed the weather and the traffic. Eventually a slick dude from Shenandoah Country Q102 took the mic and tried to whip up the burbling, diffuse crowd.

"Have you seen it? Have you been inside?" he asked, to mild cheers. He was a board member of Celebrating Patsy Cline as well, and could not let the evening pass without recitation of the legend.

"You've heard it. There were always some forces trying to keep her down. But folks, what you see here tonight, it could not have happened without people from Winchester making it happen. That's the truth!" A smattering of applause amid ongoing chatter. "And I would love for you to come visit Patsy Cline's historic house, 608 South Kent Street. That's where she was when she came home after visiting Arthur Godfrey, that night when she won, that little room. And—JudySue says it best—but she looked at her mom, with her brother sleeping right nearby. She was next to a sheet. And she said, 'Mama, it feels good to be back home. We did it.' Not 'I did it.' Patsy Cline was the American dream. And it was her and her mom.

"We gotta keep Patsy alive," he finished, while restless beer-enabled hoots began to rise from the assembled masses. "And I just say thank God we finally have something like this."

What would Julian Wood Glass Jr., let alone James Wood, have thought of their backyard being used for this kind of put-on honky-tonkin'? Not just motorcycles and country music, but Carolina barbecue? The event looked like all of Winchester's class history colliding under one tender sunset: Glen Burnie, its regal gardens, the new-money Georgian-revival museum, and a tent full of middle-class folks with no connections to the old gentry's social life, gladly tossing money at the museum and signing up for memberships. Celebrating one of their own, the first east-side woman to push beyond the life that the Woods and their ilk had designed for her. She could never have stepped foot in Glen Burnie during its height, and she was now part of the story that the Valley told about itself. She was one of the single-name demigods that this region thrived on: Washington, Stonewall, Byrd, and now, Patsy. She had brought country music out of the farm and into the city, the parlor, the concert hall, and country people followed. They were now middle class and leisure-minded, they were PR professionals and media personalities and retirees with $100 to spend on a Saturday night fundraiser.

At the edge of the festivities I saw Julie Armel, plate in hand, and remembered from the morning where I'd heard her name.

"I'll be heading up to Jim McCoy's place tonight," I told her, and she nodded in eager recognition while still chewing.

"Of course, Jim!"

"And whenever he talks about the old days, his old band, he mentions a guy named Bud Armel. Is he—"

"My husband's uncle," she jumped in. "I've never met Jim, but I have heard so much about those days and that place."

I could believe it. Bud Armel was one of those ever-present faces orbiting around Jim in black and white photos, a guitar strapped to his chest and a commanding hat upon his head. His was a name that made Jim ease back into his chair and sigh. I imagined sitting in the hearse with Bud Armel, rolling exhaustedly through the Maryland and West Virginia hill country in search of the next village roadhouse, and informing him that one day his niece-in-law would welcome a few hundred Winchesterites to Glen Burnie for a barbecue buffet in honor of Patsy Cline.

Even better, I imagined telling him that Jim McCoy would still be hosting live music on the same night. The sun was setting. I had to make the long ride back up to the place where Patsy was more than just another historical exhibit.

The sun was setting as I pulled into the Troubadour, the Christmas glow was just attaining its fullest warmth. Inside, the hubbub was considerable and the steaks were flying. The room smelled of grill grease and cigarettes. A flamboyantly coiffed blonde woman in a sparkly sequined top and black vest was slaying Tammy Wynette's "Til I Can Make It on My Own" to a backing track. When she finished, holding the final note and masterfully pulling her mic away from her mouth to manage the fade-out, she clipped it back on the stand and walked through the crowd with a smile, to the most valued seats in the house, right by the entrance, right next to Jim McCoy.

This was Sandy Uttley, from west-central Pennsylvania, and her most recent CD, *Sings the Songs of Patsy Cline*, recorded at Troubadour Studios and released by Troubadour Records in 2010, was visible on the for-sale shelves directly behind her seat. In 2011, that record won the Country Legacy CD of the Year Award from the National Traditional Country Music Association. It was the most recent feather in Jim's cap; he'd produced it and accompanied Sandy to the awards ceremony in Iowa. Tonight he looked like a trip to the post office might be an ordeal. Sandy sat down, poured herself a beer from the half-full pitcher on the table, and leaned over to hug him. A tight smile curled up underneath his trucker's hat brim. He gestured me closer to talk over the swirl of music and dinner chatter.

"Tonight we got Sandy warming up for the big show," he said in his deep, slow growl. I had to lean in close to hear him over the electronic jukebox, currently playing Garth Brooks's "The Thunder Rolls." "Carol Glass-Cooper. She's got a Patsy tribute. Brought it up from South Carolina." I could see Glass-Cooper's husband on the stage, assembling a prop WINC-branded desk, preparing for showtime.

I told Jim that I met them down at the museum, and asked if he had plans to see the exhibit.

"Oh, I'll get down there. Heard they have my microphone." I concurred. It dawned on me that I'd never asked Jim if he'd ever been to the Cline House.

"Just once, when they got it open." He paused. "It didn't look like it did. They never kept the piano there. Felt like a different place. You know Charlie'll be here tomorrow?" I'd heard. He never missed Labor Day weekend on Highland Ridge.

"We'll do 'Waltz Across Texas,' fifty years now." "Waltz" was Ernest Tubb's signature song, and every year at the Patsy birthday bash, Jim and Charlie croaked their way through it together onstage. They had now known each other for nearly sixty years, since before Charlie and Patsy became a couple. As a young man, Charlie hauled papers for the *Star*, part of a succession of odd jobs all over Winchester-Frederick County, and he loved to drink and listen to country music. It was inevitable that he and Joltin' Jim would cross paths. When Patsy and Charlie married, Jim and his first wife, Marjie, were their regular social partners, and Jim's stories from that time all revolve around getting tanked —he and Charlie so drunk they let dinner burn on the grill, or

Patsy's eyes rolling as they stayed up late, acting like loud young assholes. It wasn't until Patsy died that their friendship became one of the defining aspects of both their lives.

"After the funeral, he went back down to Nashville," Jim told me as Sandy finished her beer. "And then he would start calling me. Midnight, two in the morning sometimes. He was just looking for a friend. He'd play me records over the phone." Jim and Charlie shared the agony of Patsy's loss, but Jim had his own heartbreak happening simultaneously. After nearly fifteen years, Marjie had grown weary of his joltin'. They divorced right before Patsy's death. Jim didn't blame her; he'd had women on the road, too many to count, and always had an eye on the door, looking for the next musical opportunity rather than building a good home. He retained partial custody and his parents and sister helped watch the kids when he found gigs and sessions. And with increasing regularity, he took calls from grieving Charlie and heard the widower's favorite records.

The song that Jim most strongly associated with Charlie was recorded a few years later, in the early 1970s: Gene Davis & the Star-Routers' "I Need Help," a wailing country-gospel tune. Jim heard it for the first time over the phone, and recalled its opening lines to me now: "Here I am, on my knees for the first time, and praying is something I've never done / But Lord, I need a friend I can talk to, and I need help from someone."

This was not a well-known song, then or now, but in the growing dinnertime noise of the Troubadour with Sandy Uttley's loving hand on his shoulder, Jim recalled every word of it from memory. The way he spoke it—with all the anticipation he had in his voice for the arrival of his dearest male friend the next day—upturned the religious message, subordinating it to the interpersonal one. It sounded like a song about earthly partnership, human deliverance: "Lord, send me a friend" rather than "Lord, be my friend."

With a sudden blast, Mark Cooper cued up a backing track on stage and stood to announce "Daily Walkin' with Patsy Cline." He was dressed in a Clemson-orange embroidered stage suit and white cowboy hat. Then the side door kicked open and Carol Glass-Cooper strode in singing "Blue Moon of Kentucky," high-strutting in Patsy's famous red cowgirl getup. White Stetson, white fringed gloves.

The first act of "Daily Walkin'" was Patsy's apocryphal debut on WINC. At the wooden desk and antique microphone, Mark portrayed Joltin' Jim in this burlesque re-creation of the moment. Carol caromed through the tune, strong but unsubtle; Patsy's version is nearly conversational and tossed off, but most mortals have to exert quite a bit to hang with the melody's leaps and dashes.

"Well hello there, Mr. McCoy, my name's Virginia Patterson Hensley and I'd sure love to sing on your country show—"

The narration was ham-handed biographical roughage to move things along from one song to another. It was pure southern showbiz: part schmaltz and part white-knuckle conviction, held together by sheer gumption and the local hardware store. There has been a steady supply of Patsy tribute singers since the 1980s and 1990s, when her legend really came together thanks to *Coal Miner's Daughter*, the first biographies, and her postage stamp. Most tribute singers go the full distance with her hairstyles and outfits, and they usually perform with a narrative act just like this one, hitting most of these same details: Jim McCoy, Bill Peer, Arthur Godfrey, Owen Bradley. Jim had seen more than a few of these, and has been guest of honor at many of them as well. He claimed that he goes along with it all for Charlie—

these shows pay royalties, as does any use of Patsy's songs or like-ness. Nevertheless, he seemed unflattered by them.

"She's no Patsy. But they never are," he said to me. The au-dience around the Troubadour's tight dining room was atten-tive but not at all rowdy. Jim seemed detached, distant. He was watching a younger man's impersonation of himself yet again, watching the pivotal episode of his youth play out on an ama-teur stage—reenacted like the goddamn Civil War. Maybe if an actual Gettysburg veteran lived to see amateur enthusiasts re-create the day for fun, he would have worn the same vaguely dis-satisfied look that Jim wore that night. A memory draws power from its privacy—years of recall and revision slowly wear it down to a smaller, denser version of itself, like a dwarf star that only one person knows is there. To see it refracted back out in a mere three dimensions, rehearsed and read by two strangers, can only feel like a betrayal of its true hugeness. After a minute watching stoically, Jim gestured me close again. "Patsy had perfect pitch. She was a real musician. You shoulda heard her play the piano."

He took a long drag on his cigarette; these days, there were no short drags. His hat brim glowed orange from the fire as he inhaled. When he pulled the cigarette out of his mouth and dan-gled it over his chair back, it wobbled in his unsure hand, releas-ing a silky wisp of gray smoke that disappeared into the blur of lights along the ceiling. People from all over the world, South Carolina to South Africa, know Winchester only because of this one Saturday morning that Jim lived as a teenager. Not every man gets to watch the stage show of his own life, or see a crowd rapt and invested in it. But Jim had reason to feel depleted by it all. Back on that fateful Saturday, he was working toward his own dreams, toward something bigger than just a first-act cameo in a tribute show.

By the early 1960s, Jim had an open invitation in Nashville, where he could stay with Charlie and run around trying to sell songs and play on sessions. With hopes for a hit record, Jim left his kids with his parents or his sister and took regular trips to Music City. He would visit Ernest Tubb's Record Shop near the Ryman Theater, which doubled as a famous gathering place and performance venue for country royalty. Jim remained close with Tubb, who had ventured into retail and syndicated radio shows in the tradition of well-diversified country businessmen. With Tubb and others, Jim was brought to recording studios and back-rooms, right in the beating heart of the industry's most transformative phase. Jim watched Willie Nelson show new songs to Ray Price. He grew close with Marty Robbins. He was enlisted in pharmacy runs to buy illegal pills for Johnny Cash, which required the knowledge of certain secret handshakes. He was even brought in to observe a vocal session with Elvis himself.

These weren't just friendships and one-off brushes with stardom. Jim was known as a performer and a bandleader. In late 1962, when Patsy was preparing for a short residency in Las Vegas, the first ever by a female country singer, Jim was in Nashville to record an album with producer Tommy Hill. Hill was a veteran performer on *Louisiana Hayride,* a famed live radio country show. As a producer and record executive, he helmed pretty much every session for Starday Records, George Jones's original label, during the 1960s, and wrote songs for Tubb, Webb Pierce, and many other top-flight stars. Jim and Hill had already collaborated on a couple songs, and the buzz for Jim's upcoming record was sufficient to garner notice in *Billboard Music Week* in November. The recording went splendidly, the tapes were sent to the record pressing plant, and then—it hurts to even type it— they simply vanished. The plant lost them, then the plant went bankrupt. Jim's potential break vaporized. Then his marriage followed. Then Patsy died.

Despite the whirlwind of tragedy and disappointment, or perhaps because of it, Jim kept busier than ever in 1963 and '64. He had a regular Sunday afternoon gig at the Goose Creek Championship Rodeo in Leesburg, plus an Illinois-based manager brought Joltin' Jim and the Melody Playboys out for a tour of county fairs throughout the Midwest, where they were billed as "The Official Shenandoah Apple Blossom Festival band," thanks to their appearances there. Jim did all this while still working at Montgomery Ward and DJ-ing for WHPL, one of WINC's competing stations.

In 1964, he caught the attention of a blue-eyed waitress on Loudoun Street in downtown Winchester. Her name was Linda-Ann McPherson. She knew Jim's music and he appreciated that. He also appreciated her gorgeous face, and frankly, he was ready for a positive turn of events. They married, and had four kids in the next few years: twin girls, Penny and Angel, and two boys, James and Wesley. Jim even made another single with Tommy Hill, and partnered with the man who wrote the songs, Jean Alford, to create a label to release it, Alear Records. He sold the records in a bin in Montgomery Ward, and the store advertised autograph sessions with him. In one of his famous, oft-repeated stories, he once brought his younger kids to Nashville and took them to the Opry, where Loretta Lynn, mother of young twins herself, scooped up the baby girls and carried them onstage with her to sing. Despite a few years of setbacks and losses, Jim was moving forward with his career.

And then Linda-Ann left. Disappeared as quickly as the first Tommy Hill tape. No grand good-byes, no note, no forwarding address. To this day, none of her children have seen her more than a few times in their adult lives.

Jim was now in his mid-thirties with seven children and two ex-wives. He was still putting in the effort to get his songs in the right hands. But with Linda-Ann gone, the Nashville dream faded. To keep his gig schedule, he had to scatter the kids to the wind—some with his parents, some with Marjie, some with his sister. He'd ruined his first marriage and now his second had evaporated on him. Jim had grown up poor, but he'd always had a stable family home base, and he hated leaving his own children in such disarray. He simply couldn't make the Nashville trips with such regularity anymore, and that more or less spelled the end of his flirtation with the mainstream country record industry. Because in 1965—in great part due to Patsy Cline's success —the country record industry *was* Nashville. That was the only place to take the next step, and if you weren't there, it wasn't happening.

The only thing Jim McCoy knew how to do was play and promote country music, but he could no longer entertain a delusion of the big time: a Nudie Suit, his name in Western font spelled out in the frets of his guitar, a large band, and structurally miraculous hair. George Jones, Merle Haggard, Buck Owens, Faron Young, Ray Price: that was the summit of country accomplishment, these were the saints of the realm. And now Jim McCoy knew he would have to settle for something far south of that, something much humbler. He'd spent all his adolescence and early adulthood in blind pursuit of this one occupation and finally, after a life of running, Jim McCoy reached the one thing he'd avoided so far: a limit.

The industry was also beginning to leave him behind. In the

1960s, Nashville country matured astonishingly, absorbing and infiltrating other genres like a virus. Patsy and Ray Price introduced easy-listening strings, then Charlie Rich and Bobbie Gentry brought in R&B bass and rock guitar. By the dawn of the '70s, the Byrds were playing honky-tonk standards and Miles Davis wrote and recorded a song called "Willie Nelson."

But as an artist and songwriter, Jim knew only the Tubb model: two minutes, narrated verses, big chorus, pedal steel solo, another chorus, and out. His biggest '60s effort was "Which Away, What Away, Any Way," the bouncy saga of one man's comical search for a gal gone missin'. The rhymes are bargain-bin and his singing wobbles, but it's fabulous: pure bouncy southern showbiz. In the right label's hands, heard by the right DJ or A&R man, it might have sent Jim to another level. He might have been the next jukebox darling with decades of royalties from one big song. But by the time he released it on his own Winchester Records label in 1968, that dream had sailed on out of Jim McCoy's life, gone. He sold it in the Montgomery Ward near the cash register, and sent it out to a few regional radio stations where it received respectable airplay. And that was it. That was the cost of keeping his family together amid chaos. He hadn't had much as a young man on Highland Ridge, but he had stability. He knew where he was from and how to care for it. He had country music in his heart, but other responsibilities overruled even that. "I'm a family man," was how he'd put it years later, when I asked how come he never made the move down to Nashville permanently. He wanted a home more than a grand career. He stayed.

Now, sitting next to me, he was old, watching as Carol Glass-Cooper skipped out of WINC and her husband changed costumes to impersonate the next meaningful man in Patsy Cline's musical evolution. The role of Jim McCoy was complete. He was the first small step in a grand saga, a bit part in a friend's bigger life.

I went back up to the bar, where Codi, one of Jim and Bertha's devoted employees, was busy pouring beers and keeping track of a dozen-odd handwritten tabs. Codi was in her mid-thirties, a single mother with a young teenager, and she split the bartending duties with another woman in the same position. Saturday nights were toughest; she maneuvered between the beer taps and the lineup of rail liquor hanging in a metal basket off the coolers, with occasional stops at the yellowing cash register to ring everybody up. The most popular drink was a bright-orange concoction called Rocket Fuel: one pour of everything in a pitcher, topped off with enough Sunny Delight to make it palatable. As Carol Glass-Cooper started into "I Fall to Pieces," Codi paused from calculating another small bill in her head. To no one in particular, she said out loud, "I'm so sick of Patsy Cline."

One of the out-of-towners, a guy in an ironed polo shirt, approached the bar.

"Can I get a bourbon, neat?" he asked Codi.

"What's that mean?"

"No ice."

"Oh," she said, grabbing the handle of Jim Beam and setting a plastic cup on the scuffed bar top. "We call that a shot."

On Sunday, the novelty gun was smoking and the foil-covered casseroles were gleaming in the sun around its base. The medical-bill donation bucket was positioned by the fence door. There were only a few slow-moving, marshmallow-white clouds in the sky but everyone was still talking about rain. Jim was in his formal wear, the collared black shirt with the electric guitar pattern, and sitting near him was Charlie Dick himself, looking much younger than his seventy-nine years in dark blue pants and a light-blue button-down. The two old-timers sat in their lawn chairs, leisurely holding court as well-wishers came up for photos. They handed their babies over to Jim like he was the pope, but stayed within arms' reach.

The right ingredients were all there for the kind of legendary hoedown that all the knowing Patsy fan clubbers had prepared me for, but the whole afternoon felt somehow flat, not quite there. Maybe it was just that I'd been to one of these cookouts before, or the fact that the crowd wasn't nearly the size that I'd been told to expect for the biggest day of the Troubadour year. Boots, Beer, and BBQ was an event, whereas the McCoys' Patsy party was merely a lovely time in the open air. The pickup band was playing on the bandstand, down the hill by the tree line. They felt a mile away.

Closer to the picnic tables, the familiar sounds of hissing meat and roaring grill fire were more prominent. Codi, Little Eddie, and the rest of Jim and Bertha's young army were busy turning chicken thighs, cracking Coors Light cans, making change for $5 bills, and running plates out from the restaurant. Outside, in the light of day without loud music to distract from it, it was incredible to see how much work went into this "picnic." There is no easy way to create leisure for dozens of people. Bertha came by the grills, looking in to check on everything while Jim enjoyed his fans and his old friend.

As another ringing pedal steel intro kicked off the band's next song, I spotted Matt Hahn, Jim's doctor, up by the edge of the hill, standing alone. He was a hard figure to miss in these surroundings, a tall and upright man with a striking, pale bald head.

I clinked beers with him and we watched Jim stand up and move slowly through the crowd, accepting toasts and tributes. I asked Dr. Matt how his patient was doing.

"Jim takes the normal health equation and turns it on its head," Hahn said. "I vowed to stop him from smoking and limit the alcohol. Instead, he turned me onto whiskey. My wife and I were vegetarians when we came here, and they broke us in months."

He'd come from Washington almost fifteen years earlier, right as the new century began. Hahn's medical school scholarship mandated that he work in a needy community after graduation, so he left D.C. and headed over the hills to become a small-town family doctor, expecting to stay the minimum required time with his wife and baby daughter. Then they found that they loved it, and found a community of fellow transplants who had made a permanent home around Berkeley Springs. His practice was just over the Potomac in Hancock, Maryland, about ten minutes away. When I asked why a lifelong east coaster would raise a family in the sticks, he responded like he'd heard the question before. "It's quiet and it's safe," he explained. "And since there's not a lot of services or activities around, the families really come together and support each other. It's an actual community."

Jim McCoy was one of Hahn's earliest patients, and he knew the old man strictly on those terms until John Douglas, still years from writing the *Joltin' Jim* book, played him some of Jim's music from the 1960s.

"I was looking at these old photos that John had," he told me in the sun-dappled shade as a nine-year-old girl took the bandstand stage to sing "You Ain't Woman Enough (To Take My Man)," "and I said, 'Wait a minute, that's my patient.'" Hahn started coming to the Troubadour and, like most of us who stumble on to it from the outside, became a proselytizer. Soon their whole transplant family scene became regulars.

But Hahn became more regular than most. He had no background in country music, but he was an ex-musician. In the 1980s, during D.C.'s famously tight-knit punk scene, he fronted an antic, keyboard-heavy band called the Young Caucasians that gigged relentlessly and recorded a few albums. The more time Hahn spent with Jim, the more he learned about the man's long and occasionally merciless career in the hinterlands of the country industry, the more connected he felt to the ecosystem that Jim had created at the homeplace.

"We were one of those bands where, after every show, someone would come up and tell us, 'We're in business, it's gonna happen,' and then it never did," he told me. "And Jim was that guy in country music in the '60s."

When Jim got wind of his young doctor's musical past, his show business instincts kicked in. He smelled a hook. In 2005, he asked Hahn if he'd like to record an album: *Matt Hahn Sings the Songs of Jim McCoy.* Hahn couldn't refuse the second chance at musical glory. On weeknights after work he came up the mountain and spent hours in Troubadour Studios, working with a series of bands that Jim assembled for the sessions. Jim was not quite eighty at the time but his work ethic and energy dwarfed Hahn's own. They recorded until 2 a.m. most nights, working with local musicians who were capable but, in classic country style, only sporadically dependable. One guitar player, according to Hahn, played perfectly after eight beers but couldn't play at all after nine.

The record took two long years to make, more time than Hahn ever thought it would, and by the end of it he was practically absorbed into the Troubadour's scenery and mythology.

Jim gave him his old embroidered red suit to wear for gigs, and stood a life-size cardboard cutout of the good doctor in those radiant duds in the backroom of the bar, by the pool tables. Along with John Douglas, Hahn was now Jim's musical executor, and when Jim was inducted into the West Virginia Music Hall of Fame, Hahn accompanied him to the ceremony in Charleston. He became the unofficial mascot of the bar, proof of its gravitational force and community-building capacity, not to mention the man who was doing the most to keep Jim alive. Now, in 2013, Hahn had given a dozen-odd years—a quarter of his life—to treating and honoring Jim McCoy. No one was more surprised by this than Hahn himself.

"He brought the magic of country music to us, in such a beautiful and personal way. To rub shoulders with these people ... When we went down to see Jim get that West Virginia award, we were sitting next to Bill Withers. I'm meeting Patsy Cline's husband. And I think, 'Where am I?'"

But now Jim—his patient, after all—was faltering. He'd had stomach surgery in the spring, and was due for lung cancer tests in the early fall. What could a family doctor do for him now?

"I tell him, keep living. Have a blast," Hahn said, watching Jim walk slowly by. "At a certain point people get to dictate these things for themselves and you just try and help them out as much as possible. Out here, if someone isn't feeling well enough to come to my office, I go to them. So I'm out here a lot. And he loves music, he loves crowds. He never stops. He's got a digital studio, all sorts of gear to transfer his old tapes to CD. He had this tower built so he could start his own Internet radio station. He's got plans all the time to keep the studio active. To see someone his age working hard, making plans, using technology ... He's an inspiration."

Jim came over and whispered to Dr. Matt that it was time to go inside. Hahn excused himself and walked off through the crowd discretely. Jim followed, as did Charlie, Julie, Bertha, and a couple more of the innermost sanctum. Inside, amid only the Christmas lights and the lazily revolving ceiling fans, the old friends gathered by the bar and Bertha poured everyone a finger of Jim Beam. This was a yearly ceremonial toast, in a sense the real occasion for the Labor Day party altogether. Jim spoke to the memory of their beloved friend, mother, and widow. It was Patsy who compelled them to find this time each year, Patsy who gave shape and a soundtrack to their whole vision of the world. They'd done this toast for fifty years now, in Winchester and then up here, at the gate of the sky. Fifty years: nearly twice as long as Patsy even lived. The memory of her grew more precious with every year, because it kept everyone in touch with a sense of possibility. It was like having a friend who stayed young for life. Their empty plastic cups smacked gently on the bar.

When they reentered the daylight and the quiet potluck crowd, Jim and Charlie made their way to the stage as tradition required. Earlier in the day, Charlie had told Jim that he wasn't in the mood to do it this year but Jim responded with the guilt trump card: "I don't know if I'll be able to sing next year." So they did their duty, up the wood-slat steps and onto the bandstand. The sun was just beginning to set behind the stage; it was a punishment for the audience to stare toward it. Nevertheless, the band picked up the familiar lilting melody and "Waltz Across Texas" began. Neither of them could carry a tune anymore, but we all watched silently as these two men labored to honor each other and the woman who defined their lives.

Down on earth, at the foot of these mountains, the Museum of the Shenandoah Valley was open to visitors, charging admission to show locals and tourists just how central Patsy Cline really was to the development and history of the region. Finally the town had caught up with her, finally the local money needed her enough to pay respect. But that money wasn't anywhere near the Troubadour, and it hadn't touched Jim McCoy. He was up in the hills as he'd been for the last three decades, putting on a shoestring party and soliciting donations for his and Bertha's medical bills. Jim hadn't been granted the chance to be a mere icon; he had to go on with the messy work of the living. He had to carry the symptoms of a reckless youth into old age, and suffer the indignity of outlasting his own body. He lorded over a messy but vivid hall of memories in a world that increasingly preferred tidy museum exhibits and tourist attractions.

The sun faded behind the bandstand and the magic blue dusk settled over the party, bringing a slight cool to the breeze that fluttered the tree branches and the last of Jim's tomato plants behind the trailer. Summer was over.

5

— ✳ —

How to Build a City

A FEW MINUTES BEFORE LUNCHTIME ON
Wednesday, February 18—midday, midweek, midmonth, mid-
winter—Jeanne Mozier took her usual drive up Washington
Street in Berkeley Springs, watching her life flash before her
eyes. Entering town from the south, she passed the local historical museum, which she opened in 1984 and still operated with
only a small volunteer staff. She crossed Fairfax Street, site of the
local chamber of commerce and tourism bureau, both of which
she founded in the late 1970s. A hundred yards beyond that she
looked up at the vintage marquee of the single-screen Star Theatre, which she refurbished with her husband in 1977 and had
owned and operated ever since. And finally she arrived at the Ice
House, headquarters for the Morgan Arts Council, which she

opened right after reviving the Star, and where she still served as treasurer.

Jeanne, whose name has two syllables, went inside to grab a half-dozen white display cubes from the art gallery and brought them out to her Camry. Then she got back on Washington Street and headed south again to the Country Inn. Walking the inn's parking lot, Jeanne could see the town's namesake springs, which have flowed at a constant 74.3 degrees Fahrenheit, 1,000 gallons a minute, since the beginning of recorded time. The air outside was well below freezing. A thick steam haze danced over the four stone pools. During summer weekends the whole state-owned town square is filled with families swimming and shopping, but around Valentine's Day it was dead quiet except for the water's soft sigh.

Jeanne entered the lobby and headed for the Parkview Garden Room, the Country Inn's largest event venue and the most resplendent for many miles. In a rear corner of the room, an actual oak tree trunk, still living, was patched into the wall, a small nod to rusticity. About a hundred chairs were arranged in the center of the floor under strings of tasteful white LED globes. They faced a small stage and dais that, for the moment, were surrounded only by boxes and piles of paperwork. Running around it all was Jill Klein Rone, Jeanne's good friend of nearly four decades, and Jill's daughter, Happy. The Rone women shared the same beaming, stage-ready intensity and striking height, the exact opposite of bashful Jeanne. Together they unpacked the boxes and arranged the many dozens of entrants in this year's Berkeley Springs International Water Tasting, which was to be held that weekend. Jill and Jeanne inaugurated the event in 1991 as a way to keep the local tourism industry from hibernating throughout the cold months, but over the next quarter-century, the event grew into an industry gold standard, the so-called Oscars of Water. The title is half-facetious but there are no other contenders for it. Every year, Berkeley Springs, whose downtown is two lanes wide and a half-mile long, plays host to the most prestigious annual event of a $360-billion global industry.

Jill and Happy set aside a few bottles for the tasting itself, then left the rest to Jeanne, who brought in the display cubes and arranged them on the parquet dance floor between the dais and the audience seating. She set down the four-wheeled mechanic's dolly that her husband had bought her years ago just for this purpose, and sat upon it, moving crablike on her heels between the bottles and the cubes. Some of the water came from the springs just outside, while others had been flown in from Canada, South Korea, New Zealand, and many places in between. Jeanne grabbed the most striking ones first, like the towering plastic bottles from Oaza, a product of Tesanj, Bosnia, which featured its Berkeley Springs International Water Tasting gold medal award (from 2000, in the Packaging Design category) prominently on its label.

Oaza went on top of the cubes, then Jeanne arranged the other beauties around it. She positioned the smaller bottles into a winding barrier wall, leaving space for the pourers to walk in front of the judges' table. Over the next five hours, she carefully constructed a kind of inverse Atlantis, a small city made entirely of water. The peaks were about 3 feet high, and the wavy ends spread 15 feet across. From above it resembled a Persian tile mosaic, and Jeanne took it in from various angles, making sure it was fit for public admiration. She knew that her creation would be on regional TV by Saturday night, and on the front page of the *Morgan Messenger* on Sunday morning. As white-shirted hotel employees set up the last tables on the rim of the ballroom and

Jill and Happy double-checked the entrants list, Jeanne Mozier circled her liquid sculpture, searching for ways to improve it.

There was nothing so grand as Glen Burnie or the Museum of the Shenandoah Valley in Berkeley Springs, but this little village had undergone a history-minded economic and cultural shift of its own in the final quarter of the twentieth century, and Jeanne Mozier was very nearly the sole architect of it. Without her, this place might well have remained the same backwater that Jim McCoy left after the war, just another spot to get gas on the trip to or from Winchester. It was still that hamlet in many ways, from the grungy motel by the 7-Eleven to the Southern Belle diner just outside town, owned by one of Jim's sisters. But now Berkeley Springs was also a place to go and spend money on a good meal or a spa treatment, or even to see a world-renowned professional competition in a linen-bedecked ballroom. That kind of change doesn't happen without, as Anita politely called them in the Half Note lounge, growing pains. But it also doesn't happen without the kind of person who brings maximum effort and vision to every creative task, whether refurbishing a movie theater or aligning bottles on a parquet floor.

Jeanne drove into town from her home on the Virginia line, but if you enter Berkeley Springs from the north, from Maryland, crossing the Potomac River on Route 522 South, the approach is more dramatic and sudden. The Maryland side of 522, which runs right by the split between Interstates 70 and 68, is all broad hills and scenic woods, but in West Virginia it suddenly flattens: steakhouse billboards, twisted guardrails, and eventually, a looming, rusted-over U.S. Silica plant. Hydrogeology aficiona-

Jim McCoy at Troubadour Park on its opening weekend, June 1, 2013.

Jack Myers and his Mountain Dew-drinking macaw taking in the music at Troubadour Park.

Inside the Winchester Records recording studio, old reel-to-reel tapes are stored in the bathroom.

Ward Plaza, the site of Jim McCoy's old record store, is now just another mostly abandoned strip mall.

Closing time at the Troubadour Bar & Lounge. Jim and his wife, Bertha, share a moment.

Joe Barber and Tom Davis in their dune buggy after a night at the Lounge.

A man swims in the Cacapon River near Berkeley Springs.

The homemade champion's belt at the Covey Pro wrestling tournament.

Patsy Cline Boulevard, one of the only municipal monuments to Cline in Winchester. It's a nondescript street flanked by a Lowe's and a Kohl's.

A faded picture of Patsy Cline and a single candle mark the fiftieth anniversary of Cline's death.

Downtown Winchester (above). Apple crates line the road at White House apple processing plant (be

Oscar Cerrito-Mendoza on the newly renovated pedestrian mall in Winchester.

A location of the primary employer and healthcare provider in the region, Valley Health.

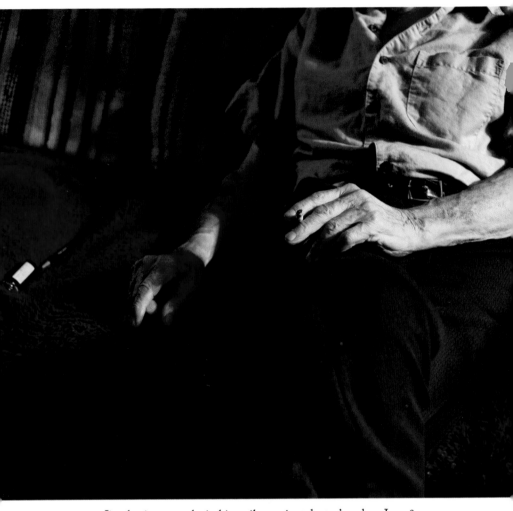

Jim, having a smoke in his trailer against doctor's orders, June 8, 2014.

dos—and there are plenty in this region—have surmised that the springs' water owes its purity and renowned flavor to the quartz and limestone ridges that the factory grinds to dust every day. But once you get to the actual Berkeley Springs town limits and the Star Theatre's cozy red-and-yellow bulbs come into view, all industrial feeling melts away, replaced by what *The WPA Guide to West Virginia* identified as "an air of peace and unconcern." For 1 square mile, Route 522 becomes Washington Street, and this dreary section of the mountains turns into a miniature stateside re-creation of an alpine sanatorium.

It was named for Sir William Berkeley, royal governor of the Virginia Colony from 1642 to 1652 and later the target of Bacon's Rebellion, the first antigovernment uprising in the American colonies. But Berkeley Springs has been famous for its supposedly curative baths for longer than Europeans have ever known of it. Native tribes traveled from the Great Lakes, the Carolinas, and the Saint Lawrence Seaway to "take the waters" here, and once Winchester and Washington, D.C., were established, it became the first American spa town. According to one long-forgotten Shenandoah Valley guidebook that repeatedly pops up, faded and broken-spined, in the region's used bookstores,

> In the early colonial times [Berkeley Springs] was a fashionable gathering place for the more sophisticated and venturesome of the east-coast dandies. George Washington and his two brothers from nearby Charles Town often went there, as did the Marquis de Lafayette, Thomas Jefferson, and Louis Phillippe, later King of France, and his two brothers during their three-year period of exile.

The author, writing in 1972, finishes his brief assessment by saying, "There were card games and dancing nightly at the casino

—now long gone." And it remained so. Even on tasting week-end, the town was dead. I drove in on Friday, February 20, pass-ing the posh private spas, antique shops, and the farmers' mar-ket site between a bank and the county courthouse. It was deep winter, so Jim's place would be quiet except for regulars, and even they might be kept away by the forecast: Berkeley Springs was bracing for 8 to 10 inches of snow over the next thirty-six hours.

Downstairs, the Parkview Garden Room was abuzz. A team from the website Water Citizen News was setting up camcord-ers and struggling with the hotel's spotty wi-fi; thanks to them, this was to be the first live-streamed International Water Tast-ing in the event's history. Other vendors were assembling their displays on the perimeter. A contractor was tightening the bolts on his taste-test rig for a high-end in-home water filtration sys-tem, while another man stood by his nonprofit's "Big Red Box," a specialized trash can meant for prescription medications, the better to keep them out of civic water supplies. There was even a life-size cartoon rendering of a superhero, Mr. Waterman, who smiled out of a water-drop face and claimed that the cure for childhood obesity was Mr. Waterman-brand Ultra-Premium Natural Artesian Alkaline Water.

The mastermind behind Mr. Waterman, brand and charac-ter both, was Taft Gaddy, a friendly and salesmanly black man who was shaking hands with everyone who so much as glanced his way. I recognized his name from the judges list; like me, he was in Berkeley Springs with two hats on. When I had called Jill Klein Rone weeks earlier to ask about press credentials, she upped the ante and asked me to serve on the tasters panel. She was prepared to flatter anyone who might write about the tast-ing at all.

Gaddy suddenly stared in awe across the room, extended

a hand, and walked up to a white-haired white man who was walking and talking with a local TV reporter.

"Are you Arthur von Wiesenberger?" he asked, and the man extended his own hand, which was decorated with a single signet ring.

"I am." His graying hair was combed into small waves behind his ears, his bright yellow tie matched his gleaming gold cuff links, and his goatee was trimmed as artfully as the Wimbledon grass.

"This is an honor," Gaddy gushed. "I've been doing this a long time, since 1989, and I started by reading your books. Can I give you a hug?"

von Wiesenberger flashed a smile like happiness had been invented only for his sake, then brought his admirer in for a brotherly embrace. Gaddy was right to genuflect—this was our godfather for the next two days, the official Watermaster of the event since its inception.

Born to a Wall Street investment banker and a part-time Hollywood actress, von Wiesenberger grew up an only child with legitimately heraldic roots: his paternal grandfather was an Austrian baron and aide-de-camp to Emperor Franz Joseph. After a childhood in New York, von Wiesenberger relocated with his parents to a family castle in Italy, where he drank local bottled water with every meal. When he returned to America—specifically Santa Barbara, to study film production—he was dismayed to discover that most restaurants served tap, which, even in toniest California, he found unpalatable: too chlorinated, too hard, too tacky on the tongue. He began visiting specialty shops to find the brands he loved in Europe, and drew the attention of Leonard Koren, publisher of the ultrahip Venice Beach monthly *Wet: The Magazine of Gourmet Bathing*, who asked him to write a column on the subject. In that capacity von Wiesenberger began reaching out to American bottled water companies to learn about the industry, which in the mid-1970s was still a niche, luxury field. His research led to his first book, *Oasis: The Complete Guide to Bottled Water,* published in 1978, when he was only twenty-five years old. As the industry grew into the U.S. behemoth it is today, von Wiesenberger's status grew alongside, until he became the unquestioned expert in the world.

In 1980, he was asked to plan and participate in the Great Bay Area Water Tasting, one of the first events of its kind in America. He canvassed San Francisco for the most expensive water he could find, then assembled a panel of interested people and relative experts. They drank and rated twenty samples from around the globe, borrowing the practices (sniffing, twirling, stemware, small sips) and even the nomenclature—think "mouthfeel"—of oenophilia, which von Wiesenberger endorses as well. He held events around the country throughout the 1980s—the decade when Evian and Fiji led the bottled water boom in America—and then received the call from Jeanne and Jill, who wanted to hold their own. They needed his gravitas. He obliged without hesitation.

In 2015, now in his late middle-age, von Wiesenberger remained an in-demand beverage-industry consultant who made regular trips to Asia to help companies identify the most pristine springs to bottle. For weekend getaways he owned a few acres just outside Sequoia National Park in the western Sierra Nevada, site of a rare naturally carbonated spring. But the International Water Tasting was a highlight of his year, and he had missed only three in the past two and a half decades.

"It's an important event in the industry. No other tasting in the world has gone on for so long. It's the benchmark," he explained to me while two hotel attendees assembled huge standing banners advertising Bottled Water Web, one of von Wiesenberger's media properties. The banners featured blonde, amply breasted models in low-cut white tank tops holding full bottles. As I leaned on a table littered with tiny giveaway buttons that proclaimed "WATER IS SEXY," von Wiesenberger thanked me for serving as a judge and excused himself with a politician's easy smile to grab a quiet booth in the hotel restaurant with the TV reporter.

After the hotel staff set up a step-and-repeat near the entrance door and the Water Citizen News crew finished fighting over the placement of their webcam, it was time for the tasting's Friday afternoon event, a four-hour seminar called "Water: Beneath the Surface and Around the Globe." There were four scheduled speakers, including this year's Lifetime Achievement Award winner, Jack C. West, chairman of the Drinking Water Research Foundation. Years ago, West had developed an exacting set of bottle-quality standards called the IBWA Model Code, after the International Bottled Water Association, which he previously chaired. He was the kind of hyper-professional who might never make it to this section of the Blue Ridge if not for a specialized tourist event.

In front of a sparse but attentive crowd, West spoke at length about the glories of bottled water and the perils of tap, revealing, for example, that municipal water supplies are responsible for "between 16 and 19 million cases of acute gastrointestinal illness yearly," a range that, for what it's worth, is conservative according to the National Institutes of Health. Bottled water, he noted, has been responsible for none, largely the result of cleaner packaging: a sterilized, FDA-approved bottle is pristine, unlike the decades-old pipes and faucet that carry your local water supply.

As West's CV and slides made clear, the tone of the Friday seminar was ripe with environmental dread and precious-bodily-fluids terror. The final speaker was Henry R. "Bob" Hidell III, 2013's Lifetime Achievement Award winner and the chairman and CEO of Hidell International, a consulting firm for beverage and nutritional companies. He was tall and wide and moved as slowly as a submarine, and at the International Water Tasting his reputation preceded him. Throughout the morning I'd heard tell of his legend: he was the foremost water expert in the world; he could divine an underwater spring without any tools at all; his blessing on a new bottling company was a harbinger of future success. Like West, Hidell was an older white man who had the stiff air and raw-chicken complexion of an early-bird dinner attendee, but with his gray blazer, black turtleneck, and penchant for grand philosophical doomsaying, he more resembled a benevolent Bond villain.

Hidell gave his entire marathon address in front of a single slide depicting a data map of the movement of human populations over millennia. He began by announcing that global warming was causing water scarcity, which in turn was causing "the beginnings of a transit of 2.4 billion people." He made cryptic reference to his forthcoming book, "a history of war," that "couldn't be published while my mother was still alive" for reasons left worryingly unsaid. Of the coming eco-social catastrophe, he warned that "except in our minds, there are no safe harbors." He explained that he'd reached some kind of Zen plane since, at seventy-five, he'd be dead before his prophecies come to pass.

By the end of his speech, when the room's atmosphere was fully pregnant with fear, one audience member sarcastically asked if there was any good news.

"Let me take a look at my notes," Hidell mumbled unsmilingly, flipping through a legal pad that he had yet to acknowledge. "No. No, I'm afraid there isn't."

His final suggestion to young people was to "find a rich girlfriend, buy land on the eastern side of Wyoming, watch the Great Plains, and make pretzels or something."

"Why not buy land in Berkeley Springs?" came a voice from the back of the room, breaking all at once the spell of unease. Our heads all turned to see who'd provided the relief.

"Thank you, Jeanne," Hidell said, with as vibrant a grin as his face could manage. He finally laughed along with everyone, though he seemed to pity us.

Jeanne stood by the exit, shaking hands and making plain that her recommendation to buy a place nearby was only as sarcastic as we wanted it to be. She was leaned against the button-covered table, smiling broadly as always. After a quick loop around the hall, checking in on the booths and helping put out small fires, she left to attend to other booster duties. The Friday night movie was only a few hours away, and she had a town to entertain.

A short while later I ventured into the freezing twilight, stopping near the steamy baths to briefly consider throwing myself in after Bob Hidell's catastrophic assurances. The water wasn't nearly suicide depth, however, just a small viaduct and a few stone enclosures around the slippery rocks where the springs came trickling out. The snow hadn't started yet but the air felt loaded with it already. The whole town glowed cobalt, speckled by streetlamps.

There is no shortage of natural beauty in West Virginia, but it was still ironic that this of all states hosted the world's biggest annual celebration of water purity. Just a few weeks earlier, in December 2014, a grand jury had finally indicted the former managers of Freedom Industries, which, the previous January, had poisoned the Elk River with 100,000 gallons of industrial coal cleaner. One-sixth of the state population—300,000 people, including everyone near Charleston, the state capital—had only foul, skin-burning liquid in their taps. Two of the Freedom honchos eventually pleaded guilty and accepted a year in jail along with heavy fines.

Within two weeks of the Elk River disaster, the independent nonprofit West Virginia Rivers Coalition released "The Freedom Industries Spill: Lessons Learned and Needed Reforms," which chastised the state's untouchable coal industry as well as shortsighted, regulation-averse politicians and an ineffectual EPA. According to the report, the spill definitively proved that "elected officials, agency heads, and members of the Legislature have made it clear that protecting human health and the environment will take a back seat to supporting lax regulation of industry." The point was made: by June, the state legislature passed a stunningly comprehensive environmental reform package headlined by new regulations on above-ground chemical storage containers like those that had ruptured and spilled into the Elk River. More than 44,000 tanks fell under the new legal umbrella.

That's when the lobbyists swarmed. The following February, legislation was introduced to the state senate that would exempt 99.8 percent of those tanks from the 2014 regulations. (A compromise eventually limited the regulations to 12,000 tanks.) In the same month, West Virginia became the first state to repeal its own existing renewable energy standard, reneging on the self-assigned duty to switch to 25 percent non-fossil-fuel power by 2025.

A few days before I went to Berkeley Springs and saw some of the most revered water on earth bubble out of the ground, a Virginia-bound CSX train carrying 109 cars of crude oil had derailed outside Beckley, about four and a half hours southwest. Two cars went into the Kanawha River. Ten others exploded at half-hour intervals. Mushroom plumes filled the sky and at least one house caught fire. Two hundred people were evacuated, and Governor Earl Ray Tomblin declared another state of emergency, this time only affecting two counties.

Berkeley Springs residents have been spared the kind of environmental disasters that plague their downstate neighbors because the eastern panhandle is separated from the rest of the state geographically, culturally, and most important, geologically. The greater part of West Virginia, including Charleston, belongs to the Appalachian Plain, snug between the Allegheny and Cumberland plateaus. This is the real sticks, land of gorgeous rolling forest that too many people see only in the credits of bleak documentaries about the Other Half, the white poor. Here's where you find places like Wirt County, population 5,901, which comes to only 26 people per square mile. Morgan County, site of Berkeley Springs and the Troubadour, is a bit denser at 65 people per square mile, but one county east, Berkeley County, is a relative metropolis of nearly 109,000 residents, 323 people per square mile. Out in the panhandle they have silica, not coal. They have D.C. within an easy drive, not rural Kentucky. They have the Shenandoah Valley within view, not the densest woods of the Mountain State.

They also have many more liberal, out-of-state transplants like Jeanne Mozier, who wouldn't be opposed to the panhandle cutting ties entirely and creating its own state based on the boundaries of the old Northern Neck Proprietary, a stretch of land belonging to Lord Thomas Fairfax in the late seventeenth century. The Proprietary encompassed everything between the Potomac and Rappahannock rivers, stretching all the way down into the Tidewater region, even a segment of the Chesapeake coast. But the bulk of it was the northern Shenandoah, Route 522's domain: Winchester and Berkeley Springs. From the very beginning of its settlement, this region was defined by its inviolability—surrounded by mountains, custom-built for farming, filled with money and cheap labor. It never became slave-powered tobacco land like the flatter, warmer areas to the east, and was never stripped for coal like the region to the west. Instead, it was defined by old money, social rigidity, bountiful wheat and apple harvests, and pristine water. In the late twentieth century, as the rest of the rural United States became wracked by economic inflation and environmental distress, the Northern Neck could be plausibly sold as a haven. And it became a destination for people like Jeanne, who had the means to relocate from denser, more environmentally compromised locations.

I walked up the road toward the Star Theatre's glowing marquee. The show that night was *The Imitation Game*, which would play at 7:30, then the same time on Saturday, followed by a Sunday matinee. The venue was a wonderful throwback: from the small lobby, visitors could either go straight through into the 350-seat theater or take a left into the tall-ceilinged concessions room, which was hand-painted by Jeanne and her husband, Jack, in a starry-night pattern and wallpapered with decades' worth of framed local newspaper coverage.

When I walked in, Jeanne was wrapping gummy worms in plastic bags to be sold for 50 cents, while Jack, sporting a handlebar mustache that could have won prizes, sat in a comfortable chair in the corner, reading the day's paper. It felt like an especially charming living room, albeit one with a vintage cast-iron popcorn maker and art deco candy-display case.

"Well, here it is," Jeanne said, rolling her eyes at her little Shangri-la. Jack smiled at her lovingly. High up to her left, in the corner above the popcorn machine, hung a large, framed black and white portrait of a young man on a motorcycle.

"That's him," Jeanne nodded toward Jack. "Nineteen sixty . . . five?" He nodded. "Five. He loves machines. When we bought the place he taught himself to operate the projector and he still does it, every show." He smiled again, looking back to the paper.

Besides that dashing photograph, the place was a museum to Jeanne. In the pictures on the wall, many dating back to the late '70s, she was slight and long-haired, her trademark asymmetrical grin peeking out from underneath massive black-frame glasses. The more recent ones showed her growing stature in the town: a clip from a national film magazine highlighted the Star's retro charm, and an article from the *Morgan Messenger* celebrated her annual role as the emcee of the Berkeley Springs Apple Butter Festival, held each Columbus Day weekend. And on the counter, above the well-lit candy boxes, sat her books.

In 1999 she published her first, *Way Out in West Virginia,* a compendium of off-kilter travel recommendations—the state's first brick road, the oldest golf course, that kind of thing. It had been recently reissued in an updated fourth edition. For her second, she coauthored the Berkeley Springs volume in the Images of America series, whose sepia-toned covers populate every small-town gift shop in the United States. So far, it is the sole book-length history of Berkeley Springs in existence; between her creation and curation of the historical museum and her authorship of that volume, Jeanne Mozier is literally the keeper of Berkeley Springs's past. When I asked her how this happened, especially since she didn't arrive here until well into adulthood, she told me that it was a message from the universe.

"When we came here in 1977, it seemed to be my cosmic assignment. 'Okay, Jeanne, here you go, this is what has to happen.'"

She didn't take celestial stuff or the sense of duty lightly. Born in upstate New York, Jeanne studied at Cornell before getting her masters in Communist Studies from Columbia. She graduated in 1967, and since "in that field, you either work for us or for them," she was soon hired as an analyst for the CIA, focused on East Asia. The Tet Offensive occurred only months into her tenure. For two and a half years, right as Jim McCoy's Nashville hopes were fading, she wrote for the agency's internal magazine and analyzed every open and undercover report that came in from Vietnam. Finally the atmosphere of spy games and brutal conflict broke her, and she went to work for the D.C. corrections system as an administrator.

While visiting an all-female jail in 1971, she witnessed a speech by an astrologer. "I watched these women," she told me while folding up plastic candy bags, "some of them were hookers, murderers—they all had the attention of a fruit fly. But when they heard this one guy speak, they were riveted for forty-five minutes. They started sharing these unbelievable psychic experiences: visions, premonitions, auras. That's when I understood the disruption on the etheric plane, the emotional chaos that surrounded these people. They had no boundaries. Some of them were certainly possessed on some level and they had no way to deal with it."

She began studying astrology with the teacher, and "it was

obvious that I had done this before. Because it was already full-blown in my mind. I predicted the day the Berlin Wall came down."

When she and Jack decided they needed to leave D.C. altogether, they got in a camper and traveled the country, stopping only in towns that had naturally occurring springs. Jeanne wanted the energy, the atmospheric power, of natural water. All around America they went, until finally, nearly back home, they landed in a little town two hours west of where they started. In Berkeley Springs, Jeanne finally felt ethereally aligned. They moved in 1977, and Jeanne convinced her friend Jill Klein Rone, a lifelong actor and theater-troupe coordinator, to move as well; Jill arrived in 1979.

Jeanne started the museum and tourism bureau, Travel Berkeley Springs, because at the time she moved in, "Nobody would've known that you could eat, sleep, and shop in West Virginia. They'd know they could hike or canoe, but hotels and restaurants are the money industries."

Her mission, the cosmic one, was to transcend the state's near-hostility to outside visitors and make Berkeley Springs the best possible version of itself, a town that took pride in its past as a leisure destination and sought to uphold that legacy. She encouraged posh private spas to open in addition to the state-owned ones that abut the springs themselves. Now, as she told me repeatedly, Berkeley Springs boasted three times as many massage therapists as lawyers. Taking a cue from the town's history of agricultural festivals in the 1930s — a new Tomato Queen was crowned annually — she founded the annual Apple Butter Festival. When his Jim McCoy record came out, Matt Hahn played with his band on the back of a flatbed truck as it crawled through downtown. Jeanne capitalized on the artist-retreat vibe by opening the Morgan Arts Council and holding craft shows on the square throughout the summer. And in order to keep the lights on in winter, she created the Berkeley Springs International Water Tasting out of whole cloth, and grew it into the town's global legacy. Because that's what small towns often are: a bunch of people gathered around a natural landmark, led by the person who wants most passionately for that landmark to mean something and make money.

Not everyone appreciated her passion, of course. There's an expression among deeply rooted Berkeley Springs folks: in this town, like so many others, it's "from-heres" versus "come-heres." One outspoken from-here, Brooks McCumbee, caused a local stir in 2014 when he posted a photo on Facebook from 1973, describing the scene "before the trash started arriving in this area." In an interview with the locally produced news website *Morgan County, USA*, McCumbee took issue with the Ice House and said, "You've got to understand, this town was a nice small town, I've lived here my whole life. We've had the city people, in a lot of cases, come in and take over. The transplants have moved in, taken over." He never mentioned Jeanne by name but she is the standard-bearer of this transformation, and McCumbee is not alone.

In her quest to rejuvenate Berkeley Springs, Jeanne had of course asked Jim McCoy to relocate down to Washington Street rather than stay stuck on top of Highland Ridge. It would be good for the hoteliers to have somewhere close to send people late at night. But Jim declined every request; relocating would defeat the whole point. The Troubadour sits on Jim's ancestral land. The McCoys have been there longer than the Star Theatre, longer than the antique shops or the silica plant, and in the business of country music, those kinds of roots mean everything. Berkeley Springs is defined by the water—so long as it's there, anything else around it is advertising. Likewise, the Troubadour is the Troubadour because it's on Highland Ridge and because it's run by Jim. He is the spring. It took decades of devoted historical preservation work and marketing effort for this New Yorker-cum-Washingtonian to approximate Jim's rootedness, and Jeanne still wasn't a local by the standards of people who knew Patsy Cline. She had single-handedly Pygmalion'd an entire town, but only an outsider would work so hard just to make a place more true to itself.

On a Friday night, however, her duties were simple: pop the popcorn, wrap up the gummy worms, and show a movie for $4.50 a ticket. Jeanne was wearing a red sweater, because "things are going into Aries—hot, fire, that kind of thing." Jack smiled. The audience would be there soon.

"You know what we call that in the industry?" asked Arthur von Wiesenberger, gesturing to the window and the heavy snow falling just outside. "Future inventory."

It was 1 p.m. on Saturday, and my fellow judges and I had assembled for our training. Most of us were media of one kind or another: the publisher of the *Observer;* the director and host of EmeraldPlanet TV, a nonprofit environmentally focused production company; a news director and on-air host for WHAG, the NBC affiliate serving the four-state area out of Hagerstown, Maryland. The last would be piping in live from the dais that night, the tasting's first-ever live-on-air television coverage.

"You'll be sitting over there," said von Wiesenberger, gesturing to two linen-covered tables under stage lights at the far end of the room, 5 yards away. "The pourers will come by and give you each water in the right numbered glass. Hold the glass up, take a look for any impurities, anything floating. Now bring the glass to your nose and take a deep breath—what do you smell? Maybe it's chlorine, or plastic. Then take a sip, and keep the water in your mouth. How does it feel on the tongue? Is it harsh or soft? Fresh or bland? As you swallow it, is it refreshing, or does it have a lingering residue?"

In all we'd be tasting sixty-seven waters throughout the day, in four "flights"—Municipal, Purified Bottled, Spring, and Sparkling. We were to rate each water in five categories listed on a specially prepared document: Appearance, Aroma, Flavor, Mouthfeel, and Aftertaste, plus Overall Impressions. The pourers would collect our papers and hand them to the scorers, who would then average the numbers. In order to keep our senses clear, we'd been asked not to wear any heavy scents or lotions. von Wiesenberger, who would only be hosting, not tasting, looked like he never left the house without a penumbra of aftershave.

"We're here today to determine what tastes good in water," he ended his introduction. "Even though we have a lot of waters here every year, it's amazing how frequently the scores line up. In general, the judges tend to like the same things, so it's clear that some waters are better tasting than others."

There was a cloth-lined wicker basket of water crackers on the table in between each judge. To our disbelief, von Wiesenberger explained that they were there in case we got thirsty. The constant flow of water, most of it heavily mineralized, could in fact wash away all our saliva over time, and the crackers were meant to help us gain a little of that spit back if needed.

We took a break as the hotel crew checked the microphones

and stage lighting. The crowd was just beginning to grow beyond the small group of Friday symposium attendees. I met a young, tweed-jacketed financier named Ben who had been dispatched from Boston by his private equity firm, which had recently purchased Llanllyr Source, a Welsh springwater company that had previously placed at Berkeley Springs in the Bottled flight. "It comes from a little town with one of the oldest inscribed stones in the British Isles," Ben explained without conviction. He pulled out his phone to show me pictures of an ancient standing rock, and I nodded as he shrugged.

At 2 p.m. sharp, the judges were compelled back to the tables and the videographer gave a thumbs-up. Von Wiesenberger joined Jill at the front of the stage, where they clicked on their microphones and instantly slipped into pitch-perfect Rose Parade rapport.

"It's the opposite of warm outside," said Jill, "but it's so warm in this room, and you all are a big part of that. And now I'd like to introduce my good friend, he's been with us almost every year since we started this long ago, Arthur von Wiesenberger!"

To my left, one of my fellow judges, the middle-aged male publisher of the *Observer*, took a bite of a cracker and looked wistfully out toward the crowd. "God, you could do anything with that name."

"You know, it's so cold outside," von Wiesenberger said with a leer, "that I heard Congress couldn't even get in a heated argument." A groan rolled over the room like a soft wave.

"And just like we say every year," said Jill, before von Wiesenberger joined and they chanted in unison, "*Let the waters flow!*" The pourers came out with unmarked carafes and gave us half a glassful of each water in the flight. These were the Municipal waters, the common stuff from the sink, sent in by little towns like Berkeley Springs that were proud of their local supply and looking for recognition.

I was as skeptical as anyone as I stuck my nose in that first glass and sniffed embarrassedly. I smelled a weak hint of chlorine, and then took a sip and sensed it on my tongue as well. It was nothing worse than what I'd expect from the tap at home, and I judged it accordingly, giving it a 13 out of 14 in the Overall category.

But after a half-dozen other samples, I realized just how forgiving I'd been. Some of them felt like chilled silk. I wanted more of them, immediately. We'd been instructed not to react to the water so as not to sway our neighbors' opinions. We weren't supposed to look at each other's forms, either. The audience, about twenty or thirty people by this point, sat in silence. It was as if someone had consciously designed the bizarro Troubadour—a stage, a dance floor, low ceilings, and entertainment, but in every meaningful sense the opposite of a place that called itself "Hillbilly Heaven." There were large bright windows instead of the smoke-filled air of Jim's main room, fresh water and crackers rather than beer and onion rings, live-streaming video instead of a mile-high cell-phone dead zone. And most horribly, the "show," as it were, consisted of a would-be baron in a suit telling awful jokes while a bunch of come-heres sipped water from crystal and wrote calmly, betraying no emotion whatsoever. No one who grew up in this part of the world would have settled for such a waste of a dance floor. But no one in the audience had grown up in this part of the world.

The second flight, Purified Bottled waters, were the hardest to judge since they were virtually indistinguishable from one another. These were simply tap waters that had been run through industrial-grade Brita filters. If Dasani or Aquafina or the plastic jug in your doctor's waiting room had been competing, this is where they would have been. I couldn't tell one from another, and assigned them all a generous grade.

A break followed, and I walked into the growing crowd to see just who would travel to the snow-covered Blue Ridge foothills for an event like this. I found two serious-looking young men, John and Travis, who had come down from New Salem, Pennsylvania, where they founded Life Source Water Service in 2008. They now delivered bottles to homes and offices around a 45-mile radius in the south-central portion of the state. I asked why they'd bother entering the contest.

"I guess a lot of people would say it's bragging rights," said Travis shyly. "But really we entered just to see where our water stands." They had recently purchased a new warehouse office and had two trucks making deliveries. The golden Berkeley Springs seal would be some kind of boon, even if they didn't quite know what sort.

Two other men, middle-aged cousins, had come from suburban Toronto representing their own, even greener business, Theoni Natural Mineral Water. They were Greek, and nearly two decades ago had discovered that their family land in the small central town of Vatsounia contained a natural spring.

"I'm a businessman," explained Jim Williams, the company president. "I've worked in finance, tire wholesale, and I own a silencer manufacturing company, and we knew we had a good product here." It took years of wrangling with the Greek government but they finally opened their bottling plant in 2013, and they weren't bothering with local service.

"The model is Evian," he said. "We have geologists checking the water flow, we're talking with distributors in Asia. We just came back from a food and beverage conference in Abu Dhabi. Last year we beat Fiji and Evian at the European water awards." He was referring to the 2014 International Taste and Quality Institute awards, where Theoni had received a rare three-star rating in its first year of evaluation.

"But it'd be the best thing in the world to win this," Jim said, gesturing around the tiny ballroom, where, outside, the snow was growing heavier, raining down in thick specks against the deep red light of a SHEETZ sign.

The judges had been asked to wear fancy dress for the post-dinner events, the better to honor the bigger-ticket water in the evening flights. I went up to my room and changed into my suit and tie with the TV on, watching commercials for car dealerships and banks in Hagerstown, Maryland, about 45 miles northwest. In both cases, a pretty-enough female employee spoke directly into the camera and gave just the slightest sultry edge to deals on trade-in values and low-interest home loans. From my window I could look out across the snowy parking lot to the intersection of Johnson's Mill Road, the route up to Jim and Bertha's. Eight to 10 inches was a threat for those of us in town, just a couple flat miles from Interstate 70. I grew nervous thinking of that storm hitting elderly, infirm people in a trailer on a mountaintop. On the television, another young woman in unflattering lighting was warning us about the road conditions. I used the bathroom three times in thirty-five minutes.

When I reentered the lobby, the locals were now arriving in force. Full families came in at once, thumping chunks of snow off their boots onto the carpet. The children immediately unzipped their coats and wriggled out of them like shedding snakes before sloppily running from exhibit to exhibit, guzzling water samples and shadowboxing Mr. Waterman. Their parents gathered up the spent jackets and collapsed into audience chairs, unzipping their parkas and slowly unwinding their faded scarves with long, exhausted sighs. Once situated, they were more talkative and excited than any of the industry people in attendance, and the place began to dance at last. The parents looked grateful for the excuse to leave the house. They spoke zealously about everything, from the blizzard and the cold to the preponderance of suits and, of course, the 15-foot winding sculpture of bottles that sat ostentatiously on the parquet. Besides hats and coats, most of the from-heres had brought large reusable shopping bags, since the highlight of this spring-addled town's winter every year was the "Rush," a free-for-all where the public was able to grab whatever exotic water bottles they could from the floor. Jeanne's little city wasn't only showmanship—it was a gift to her neighbors, a little handout for residents to partake of the bizarre global bounty that somehow found its way to their backyard. A thank-you, as well, for sitting through a water tasting as if were actual entertainment.

At 6 p.m., our hosts resumed, unafraid to reuse material for the newcomers.

"You know, Jill," said von Wiesenberger, "it's so cold out there that I heard Congress hasn't even been able to get in a heated argument."

Like affectless game-show models, the pourers emerged with their carafes, wearing all black. As before, light piano music played through the room's sound system New Agey covers of Motown songs and movie themes. There was more human noise in the room and more enchanting clothing onstage, but the same worry nagged at me while I began sipping and sniffing again: Why would anyone watch this? As if on cue, the TV cameraman set up to our right gave a 3-2-1 finger countdown and one of my fellow judges, the Hagerstown broadcaster, gave his live report from the dais. The side of my head was now on the same show I'd been watching minutes earlier between pee breaks. I tried to focus on the task at hand.

Many of the waters in the Spring flight smelled earthy and mineralized, almost like a wet cave. These were the most prestigious waters, the single-source, untreated spring products like Theoni and Llanllyr Source. They all felt airy on my tongue, even more luxurious and flavorful than the best of the Municipal samples. They tasted cold even though they weren't. These waters were a brand of natural miracle to match Shenandoah apples. Halfway through the forty samples, I hit upon a few in a row that tasted relatively unimpressive, and I wondered if I'd simply gone numb. Then I took my next sip and had that same epiphanic experience that the best ones earlier in the flight had provided. I wasn't quite ready to adopt the full von Wiesenberger lifestyle—he said his children never once drank tap, and that his dog preferred Perrier—but I could understand the appeal. To have every sip of water in your life safe from contaminants, chemical treatments, industrial disaster, or even plain flavorlessness—it was more of luxury than I'd ever previously considered, and the far-flung origins of all these natural beauties really underlined just how few people enjoy it on a regular basis. If that were all Berkeley Springs afforded its residents, it would be a considerable benefit to living there.

The final flight was twelve Sparkling waters, a cruel joke considering our stomachs were now filled with the fifty-five previous sips. I figured each taste had been at least 3 or 4 ounces, meaning we were nearing 2 gallons on the afternoon. And here came CO_2, like a final sprint uphill.

But this wasn't your average grocery store seltzer. The bubbles were delicate and fine, like champagne, and a few of the samples barely tasted carbonated at all. But that also meant they were light, crisp, and less harsh, with more room for the actual mineral flavor to shine through. They all tasted less lab-born than any sparkling water I'd ever had, and a few were indeed naturally carbonated, from rare springs like von Wiesenberger's in the Sierra Nevada.

After my last sip, I was ready to sprint for the bathroom, but there would be no quick movements. The Parkview Garden Room was now a party: more people, less businessman stiffness, the windows black except for torrents of snowfall. And since the lobby bar was now open and serving, nobody seemed to care about water, only red wine. The room twinkled with clinking glasses. Between the threatening weather, the free-flowing alcohol, and the hanging strings of lighting, the whole event finally achieved something like the Troubadour's air of improbable decadence—a luxury water tasting competition, in the snow, in a town smaller than a midsize concert hall? Why not? There's an actual Patsy Cline gold record right up the road.

Jim Williams and his cousin canvassed the room, wearing matching Theoni sweatshirts and passing out half-liters to everyone. The Pennsylvanians were sitting by themselves, silent, buzz-cut and unmoving, as they'd been the entire day. I noticed Bob Hidell, the doomsday prophet of water consulting, sitting next to his much younger, wine-sipping wife. His arms were crossed, and he made no movements other than the bouncing of his lower jaw as he lectured a rapt man nearby. They were three of the only unsmiling people in the room.

Jill Klein Rone consulted offstage with the webcam team and then clicked on her microphone to kick off the awards-giving portion of the evening. But it began with her summoning of "the woman who put Berkeley Springs on the map." Jill extended a loving hand as Jeanne Mozier ambled past her bottle sculpture and up to the stage amid applause.

Jeanne took the microphone and the volume throughout the room dropped. She had no stage voice and no notes, just an earnest message for the folks who'd come out for this perennial ecosystem she'd cultivated. "Now I know this is the Oscars of water and everything," she said, "but this year we are actually happening on Oscar weekend and we have a connection to them. One of our purified waters, IndigoH2O, is going to be in every gift bag at the Academy Awards tomorrow night!" Applause for the validation that our little mountain party was worthy of Hollywood. "And I'll tell you something, I spoke with the owner of Indigo today and he said he'd be more excited to win the Berkeley! Springs! International! Water! Tasting!"

By now I could actually feel the crowd encroaching on the free bottles. Sitting in the second row, I could barely see through the wall of jostling sweaters and empty bags. And at this worst possible moment, the time came for the presentation of Jack West's Lifetime Achievement Award. Jill and Jeanne cued up a DVD tribute to the water-purity enthusiast as a groan of impatience rose from the tittering crowd. The TV was too small for most people to see, the volume too low for most people to hear, and it took an interminable minute or so for one of the hotel's AV guys to fix a technical glitch with the DVD player itself. Finally, after the staid video tribute, West came onstage to accept his tear-shaped crystal award, and the audience clapped perfunctorily, talking among themselves.

Jill and von Wiesenberger reclaimed the microphones and reinstituted the air of glamour.

"Hamilton, Ohio!" Jill announced the Municipal winner, scanning the room to see if they'd sent representatives. No such luck. A great cheer erupted anyway, celebrating the very idea of small-townishness and the simple luxury of perfect water. Some faraway borough in the Midwest now had a claim to renown to put on their town sign, and what could be more worthy of celebration?

For the Spring awards, I watched Jim Williams, now seated, tapping his fingers anxiously on his knees. One by one Jill counted down the runners-up and medalists from Australia, Canada, Tennessee, and California, before announcing that the winner came from Greece. Jim's fingers curled into a fist.

"Fengari Platinum, from Athens!" she shouted, with an even less hopeful look around to see if anyone was there. Jim and his cousin stood and clapped heartily for their countrymen. Ben, whose Welsh client had also failed to place, took a sip of red wine and laughed from his perch among the "rushers."

Athens won again in the Sparkling category. "Daphne-Ultra Premium Quality Natural Mineral Sparkling!" she read slowly from her card.

Travis and John stood with their arms crossed, exchanging an occasional nervous glance as Jill began the Purified awards. They were not among the runners-up; again, it came down to the gold. It would be all or nothing for Life Source.

"It's Indigo! IndigoH2O, Berkeley Springs scoops the Oscars!" she exclaimed, and we all cheered.

The competition over, Arthur von Wiesenberger explained the Rush rules: "First, no pushing and shoving. We have young children here. And adults who act like children." He paused for a laugh that never had a chance. "Second, remember there are glass bottles. Please be respectful . . ." Then his voice, amplified though it was, was lost in the din. I hopped through the mass of eager water-gatherers and found one of the pourers on the other side of the room. I asked him how worried I should be.

"Oh, well, this is pretty mild. Few years ago we had a man in the front row fall over as the Rush kicked off. Turned out he was only drunk, but another time, a woman with a walker got pushed over and trapped against the floor while people filled their bags." I held my breath as our hosts completed the countdown.

But this year's Rush was nearly chivalric. As Jill and von Wiesenberger shouted "*Go!*" a hush fell. Kids led the way, running up to the edges and eagerly grabbing the lighter plastic bottles. Glasses gently clinked, cameras flashed. Grown men and women were soon down on their knees, checking each bottle before putting it back or loading up. Everyone stepped calmly and deliberately, and even a few bagless attendees jumped in to claim as many bottles as their hands could hold. In quiet excitement they set about dismantling Jeanne Mozier's little city, reducing five hours of careful work to an empty floor with a half-dozen tipped-over display cubes strewn about. She watched it from a spot against the wall, as far from the crowd as one could be in a tight ballroom. This was perhaps the most important part of her weekend. Everyone else—the Greeks, the Pennsylvanians, the judges with their distant bylines and search for the next local-color story—would be leaving in the morning, but the people with grocery bags were her neighbors. These were the people she counted on to support her museum, her art space, her movie theater. They might have mixed feelings about her monopoly over the Berkeley Springs social and economic reality, or maybe they'd heard whisperings about her previous life in Washington, D.C., and the Ivy League—something about communists? A little water could go a long way, especially in a place that knows how to appreciate it. How else but through Jeanne would the families of Berkeley Springs get to taste $15-a-bottle water from Australia, Thailand, or the Baltics? How else might their adorable snowbound children end up as charming interviewees on the evening news? Maybe it was worth it to trust her after all.

Jeanne had already e-mailed out the press release announcing the winners of this year's International Water Tasting. Industry representatives all over the world would awake to the news that a small historic spa town in West Virginia had the inside track on the Academy Awards. The release quoted Arthur von Wiesenberger: "It was another wonderful year for the longest running and largest water tasting in the world. Berkeley Springs is the granddaddy of them all."

The hotel staff opened the ballroom doors as the kids pulled their barely dry coats back on and their fathers hoisted strained bags over their shoulders. The families marched home in the cold quiet, through streams of thick snow and wide circles of pale streetlamp light. Like Dr. Matt Hahn said, the streets were quiet and safe, and the community had in fact come together on a snowy night and made a private party unlike anything you'd find nearby, or even in a richer place over the Maryland or Virginia lines. For a few hours at the Country Inn, Berkeley Springs resembled the regal idyll that history books describe. But plenty of the parents walking down Washington Street that Saturday night had lived there before the International Water Tasting was even a from-here's vague notion. For them, "America's first spa town" might as well have been Tombstone or ancient

Rome. They'd grown up in a lonely mountain town with incredible water, low property values, and a few good places to drink cold beer. They'd known a river nearby and a great rusted factory even nearer. A night of white linen and red wine might have been lovely, it may have even had the patina of history, but that isn't the same as feeling like home.

6

Toxically Pure

THE WINCHESTER WALKING MALL LOOKED ex-
actly as it was meant to. The late-morning sun beamed off storefront windows and reflected in the sunglasses of ambling middle-aged men in brewery T-shirts and baseball hats. They walked
side by side with their wives, glancing around without urgency
as they waited to meet their children for brunch during a visit to
Shenandoah University on the other side of town. From a bay
window seat in a dimly lit, earth-toned coffee shop, I watched
these couples shuffle along, past restaurants where young male
employees were putting out *al fresco* seating. Past a few black-
clad teens squinting into the bright sky, trying their best to look
wayward while in sight of a half-dozen antique shops. All the
way to the walking mall's broad black gate, on which OLD TOWN
WINCHESTER blared in white letters on painted steel. Piccadilly

141

Street, the intersecting road, looked dead. But the walking mall bustled.

If the one-night water tasting and modest theater embodied Berkeley Springs's economic evolution, this stretch of restaurants and retail boutiques embodied Winchester's. This, like Jeanne Mozier's many innovations and businesses, was designed with out-of-towners in mind. It was made to give visitors and tourists something to do and somewhere to eat when they inevitably exhausted their Civil War or parents' weekend activities. Loudoun Street, location of the walking mall, used to be the place where Patsy's people parked their cars and hollered at each other in the moonlight while passing a bottle. Now it was lovely, clean, wholesome. Capital investment will do that; Old Town Winchester has been treated to more than $125 million in funding since 1985. That kind of money will buy a lot of smooth brick. That kind of money will bring espresso to the upper Valley.

In 2007, a middle-aged Winchester native named Joe Bageant wrote a scathing essay about the walking mall and its deadening tourist-trap charm. He described the very coffee shop where I was sitting as the town's "obligatory Starbucks knockoff," and that was one of his kinder judgments. The occasion for his essay was Winchester's First Friday celebration, where the shops stayed open late and enticed buyers with wine and spreadable cheeses. Joe attended with his wife, Barbara, and came away haunted as usual:

> A well dressed woman, one of our many Yankee transplants, stands nearby gabbing about why she chose a certain artificial condo development called "Creekside Village," a development more or less embedded in a shopping center at the edge of town, as opposed to others as far as a mile from a

mall. What more could a person ask for in life than to [live] within walking distance of Jos. A. Bank, and Ann Taylor? . . . Anyway, Mall Locked Village would have been too obviously accurate a name, so the pretense that a creek once filled with crawdads is still there was probably a better choice. I cannot help though, but remember the old wetland where the red winged blackbirds perched on the cattails and sumac branches, piercing the muggy stillness of summer, issuing their crystalline cry before lifting off to nudge the sky with their bold red shoulders.

At the time he wrote this, Joe had just published his first book, an essay collection called *Deer Hunting with Jesus*, which was full of similarly crestfallen threnodies that made Winchester sound like the evil nexus of a permanently corporatized, fallen world.

His hook was that he spoke as an insider, a leftist skeptic who also knew the white underclass world—the Troubadour side of the equation, including the Troubadour itself—firsthand. Born in 1946, Joe left Winchester as a young man to travel and write throughout the West. He returned right as the country elected its second President Bush, having convinced Barbara, his third wife, that the move would calm them after years of uninspiring professional jobs in suburban Oregon. Instead, their relocation knocked something loose inside Joe. Drinking at his favorite dive bars—working-class holes like Coalie Harry's and the Royal Lunch, across the street from the George Washington Hotel—he reconnected with some of the people he knew as a young man. And to Joe's surprise, the old gang was mostly terrified and enraged. They thought everything was turning against them.

He gradually lost his corporate air and grew feral. He dressed in old work clothes and grew his beard out again. At karaoke nights and in the 7-Eleven parking lot, Joe listened to his people despair over their menial jobs, health-care debt, and the liberal media. He was disgusted by his friends' closed-mindedness, but their world-consuming panic infected him. He saw it all on a historical continuum: the old First Family and orchard-owner classes were now slumlords and land developers, and a new crop of wealthy outsiders had come to town bearing ciabatta and craft beer that few locals could afford.

Deer Hunting garnered a six-figure advance and blurbs from Studs Terkel and Howard Zinn. It led to speaking invitations in England, Italy, and Australia, where Joe shared stages with leftist figureheads like Thomas Frank and Barbara Ehrenreich. His ideas were quoted approvingly by the *New York Times,* NPR, and the BBC, particularly as the 2008 presidential election neared. In his seventh decade, Joe Bageant was suddenly the last thing that a shitkicker from the lower rungs of Valley society was ever expected to be: a public intellectual.

And in everything he wrote, he made clear that his observations about inequality, the death of regionalism, and bubba culture were all grounded in his hometown. "Like most modern Southerners who've fled their native states for long periods of time," he wrote in 2004, in the first piece to appear on joebageant.com:

I have the standard love/hate relationship with my home town—Winchester, Virginia. On one hand, it is a backward and mostly irrelevant place where the question of whether Stonewall Jackson had jock itch at the Battle of Chancellorsville still rages right alongside evolution and abortion. To be sure, it is the standard venal Southern place, where poverty and ugliness are thrust into one's face daily, with all the gothic family melodramas of greed and intrigue so often written about [in] Southern novels. On the other hand, it is the place that made me who I am, a moralizing, preachy and essentially lazy bastard who likes to drink.

With the exception of Willa Cather, who was born in nearby Gore, Virginia, no writer from the area ever achieved the level of fame and influence that Joe Bageant did in the first decade of the twenty-first century—and Cather barely wrote about the Valley. Joe, by comparison, elevated it to a personal Rosetta stone for his understanding of what had gone wrong with his country and his species.

Through the coffee shop's glass I saw a middle-aged blonde woman approach and knew instinctively she was my appointment for the morning, Barbara Dickinson herself. She'd lived in Winchester for fifteen years, but you could tell she was from outside. Her ranginess and cautious friendliness marked her as midwestern, originally from Wisconsin. Barbara set her crinkled brown shopping bag down and went to the counter for her coffee. When she got back with a wide mug, she pointed out the leaf pattern in her latte foam.

"Here's how you can tell D.C. is creeping in," she said. "We have baristas now."

Sitting in the coffee shop, Barbara and I were about two blocks south of the colonial that she and Joe lived in during his transformation, a big ramshackle palace with a pillar and a porch on a corner lot. It was right next to the Stonewall Jackson House, the general's residence during the Civil War, now a museum. There was a semi-stunned quality to her voice as she discussed the *Deer Hunting* years, like Joe's anger had ambushed them both.

"He came back with all this hope, these memories," Barbara told me, stirring her coffee. "He had created this wonderful environment in his mind—and there are some very nice people here —but that anger kept bubbling up. Coming back and seeing all this inequality was just . . . too much."

If Jeanne Mozier's benevolent takeover of Berkeley Springs represented the feel-good version of the upper Valley's recent cultural transformation, Joe Bageant was the most vivid chronicler of that transformation's psychic toll. In a place as historically self-sustaining as Winchester–Berkeley Springs, the sudden influx of outsiders that started in the 1960s and 1970s represented a true cataclysm, and everywhere you go you still see the fallout from it. The arrival of Joe's reviled Creekside Village—like the arrivals of Walmart's megastore and the Rubbermaid factory— showed that the chamber of commerce was more concerned with attracting the right kind of outsiders than improving the lives of people who were already there. A new walking mall doesn't make a working person's life any easier, but the gradual loss of long-standing businesses can make them feel frightened and powerless. Joe knew they weren't wrong to feel this way. He had managed to escape the working class and still felt this way himself.

Barbara pulled the brown bag out from under her chair and started searching through the makeshift archives that Joe had left behind. I wondered how she lived in this place without him, how she forgave it for the pain it caused her. But maybe without Joe's bleak, unceasing harangues sullying the air around her, Barbara was exactly the kind of sunny out-of-towner who could love Winchester without complication. She could see that a place like this coffee shop was in fact perfectly comfortable and welcoming, and that any town would be lucky to have a walkable strip of decent food and tchotchkes next to a stunning library.

She chose a couple of photo albums from the bundle of manila folders and scribble-filled notebooks. Outside, beyond the window behind her, the walking mall stirred. But the pictures on these stiff pages recalled an earlier, gruffer Winchester, when Loudoun Street was still a place where farmers and housewives shopped. Joe had put these albums together with no allegiance to chronology, so snapshots of his mid-'60s beatnik phase sat next to others of his three kids, twenty-five years later. There were a few of his father, but only in old age, and nothing at all from Joe's earliest years, because that life didn't include cameras.

He was born on Highland Ridge in 1946, a few miles south of where young Jim McCoy was just coming into his own as a guitar player and hitchhiker. Joe knew the family land on Shanghai Road as "Over Home," a place where generations of Bageants had grown, picked, and preserved their own vegetables and slaughtered their own hogs, all without modern machinery or vehicles. In a memoir, *Rainbow Pie,* written after *Deer Hunting with Jesus* but never published in America, he described his childhood as "anachronistic even in the 1950s . . . charged with folk beliefs, marked by an ignorance of the larger world, and lived unselfconsciously under the arc of Jeffersonian ideals."

The only currency in such a life was work, "calories burned." Joe estimated that his grandfather never made more than $1,000 a year, but the family lived plentifully on only a few acres of vegetables, a small stock of animals, and deeply ingrained wisdom about the management of each. Highland Ridge was dotted with similarly rooted families, including the McCoys. They patronized the same general store for staples and relied on each other for the rest of their worldly needs, like a truck to haul the tomato harvest to the nearest cannery. It was "a system where everyone benefited through an economy of labor," Joe wrote in *Rainbow Pie*, "with the small money of small farmers supplying the grease for the common-sense machinery of community sustenance." And even before Joe was old enough to join hunting trips with his daddy and uncles, it was doomed.

All those Byrd-beloved postwar agricultural regulations made quick work of hill-country enterprises like the Bageants' and McCoys'. New highways and corporate subsidies gave large-scale manufacturers an advantage over family farms. It took barely a generation for rural Americans to adapt, and soon they were completely ensnared by corporations. They started working for the same people who had put them out of business, typically on assembly lines or by "driving truck."

In the late 1950s, Joe Bageant Sr. had a teamster's salary coming in and a big rig that made mountain driving unfeasible. So he took his wife and children to the city and left Over Home to the grandparents. The Bageants' arrival in Winchester was really a homecoming, since the family name had been there as early as 1751, but they weren't welcomed warmly. The town was still Byrd territory through and through. Joe would later claim to have mowed Harry Flood Byrd's lawn as a teenager, though he had a lifelong fondness for suspiciously unverifiable stories, particularly regarding brushes with celebrity. By various friends' accounts, he was babysat or given a toy or sung to by Patsy Cline, who was still returning to South Kent Street in between recording dates and unglamorous shows when the Bageants came to town.

Whether or not he actually cut the senator's grass, Joe was immediately affected by the stark class division that Byrd and his ilk embodied and enforced. His father quit trucking and took up repair work at an auto shop, but money remained tight. The Bageants moved whenever they fell behind on rent, which meant they moved constantly. Even as a teenager, Joe sensed that their relocation to the city had cost them more than just a place on ancestral land. His mother was repeatedly hospitalized for depression, and his father, a locally renowned laborer whose own manual work had once been enough to fill his three kids' bellies, now struggled to keep their bedroom heated. Joe so pitied his father that he didn't even hate the man for taking the shame out on him with a belt.

Bad at school, bad with girls, beat at home, he found refuge at the Handley Library. Joe would often skip school to pursue what he called a "marvelously undirected pursuit of the mind" consisting of everything from *Boy's Life* to Pericles's orations, Civil War diaries, and *Native Son*. He also painted well enough for a mail-order art school representative to visit one of the Bageants' many addresses and offer a scholarship covering two-thirds of the course's tuition. Joe, then thirteen, offered to pick up an extra paper route to cover half of the remainder, but his father still had to decline. That last $50 was too much for the family to bear on a car repairman's wages.

This was how Joe learned about the shame of poverty. Not material lack—the subsistence life on Shanghai Road had certainly been dollar-poor—but the brutal reality of a sixty-hour work week for non-negotiable pay that barely covered life's necessities, let alone your son's blooming artistic dream. It was the unfair terms of the struggle that stuck with Joe, the fact that wealthier people had pushed his family off the farm, then kept them in a chokehold when they landed in town.

Like Jim McCoy, Joe cultivated dreams of escape, and leapt at whatever unglamorous opportunities presented themselves. Joe dropped out of school, lied about his age, and joined the navy at age sixteen, serving noncombat time aboard the USS *America*. His military career was only just long enough to secure VA benefits, but when he returned home he found a beautiful country girl named Cindy. Her tight curls hung around her face like a halo. And then, like a revelation: acid. He first tripped in 1965, right as Julian Wood Glass Jr.'s reimagining of Glen Burnie was in full swing, and poignantly, Joe received his first dose "thanks to my gay friend George, who was being 'treated' for his homosexuality with lysergic acid and enjoying every minute of treatment." As an adult, Joe called LSD "the Promethean spark of whatever awakening I have managed to accomplish in this life . . . For the first time in years, my life in that small town was very enjoyable."

Joe soon became involved in a "small psychedelic scene, one among thousands in heartland America at the time." Such a group would have shopped at the record store that Jim McCoy opened in Ward Plaza in the mid-'60s, where he would typically respond to young people's requests for the Beatles by recommending cornpone truffles like Jim Reeves's "Roly Poly." Jim abstained from drugs all his life, the result of watching fellow musicians and working men destroy themselves through every pill, pipe, and powder they could manage. Perhaps he recognized the particular glint of these young hippies' eyes, or even admired what local officials referred to as their "suspicious happiness."

Eventually, the Winchester Christian class couldn't abide the underground psychedelic resistance anymore, and Joe was the inaugural victim of the crackdown. He claimed for years to have been Winchester's first marijuana arrest, and also said that he lived in Resurrection City, a short-lived social-justice commune in Washington, D.C., while awaiting trial. This dates the ordeal to summer 1968, meaning he was already a father; Cindy gave birth to Timothy, named for Leary, in 1967. Joe was acquitted but the experience shook him. He knew he couldn't keep his young family and newly expanded consciousness locked in Byrd country anymore. In 1969, he and Cindy escaped in a school bus, hayseed flower children set free.

At the time, Boulder, Colorado, was teasingly referred to as The Buckle of the Granola Belt, and indeed there might as well have been a dog whistle blaring on Pearl Street, beckoning the nation's dropouts and longhairs. The open sky and relative seclusion had attracted everyone from the Weathermen to the Nitty Gritty Dirt Band to Allen Ginsberg. The nearby Pygmy Farm, one of the innumerable rural communes spread across America at the time, hosted visitors like Chögyam Trungpa, the Buddhist scholar who loved the area so much he stayed, founding Naropa University and the Shambhala Meditation Center in 1974.

Joe and Cindy pulled in after nearly a year of extensive travel in the bus, and their ultimate goal was still San Francisco. But the Rockies felt like kismet. Joe liked to say—again, unverifiably—that they pulled into Boulder on the inaugural Earth Day, April 22, 1970. The atmosphere of Buddhism, banjos, and Beat poetry made San Francisco seem unnecessary.

The mood in Boulder was high-minded in every sense, but Joe was the son of a laborer with a son of his own, so he wasn't averse to serious manual work. At one point, moving boxes at a grocery store, his back gave out. Laid up in the hospital, Joe began to write. He shared a poem when his friend Jerry Roberts came to visit, a "Howl"-indebted portrait of Boulder's nightlife scene. Jerry made copies of the poem and posted them around the city. When he was discharged, Joe reentered a city that had been plastered with his words. They were un-bylined, but the thrill jolted him. After an adolescence that had been marked and saved by books, he suddenly realized he had a literary voice. And after years in a place where worth was dictated by money and bloodlines, he was living somewhere that welcomed his mind.

Using raw talent, enthusiasm, and all available drugs, Joe willed himself into a writing career. He began scrounging freelance assignments, writing features about local characters and touring musicians for the *Colorado Daily*, *Rocky Mountain News*, and other regional venues. His steadiest work came with a Boulder-based ersatz *Rolling Stone* called the *Rocky Mountain Musical Express*. Joe was its main editor by 1977, though he was so prolific a contributor that he often ended up filling issues with his own work under multiple pseudonyms. He interviewed the Naropa people, Burroughs and Ginsberg, Hunter Thompson (then living in Aspen), and Timothy Leary. He profiled drug smugglers, car thieves, Karen Silkwood's attorney, and Colorado's last remaining cowboys. One freelancer, a former bassist for ? & the Mysterians, visited the Bageant trailer home to deliver a draft for the upcoming issue. He was a new writer himself, and in the course of a pep talk about the craft, Joe handed him a copy of *The Elements of Style* and a bag of speed. Then he sent his protégé back into the world with assurance: "If you want to write, here's what you need."

He also traveled prodigiously. With Cindy and Tim he saw

Belize and Mexico in 1975, and he took a musical pilgrimage to Memphis with Jerry around the same time. Most affectingly, Joe started taking road trips with the *Express*'s distributor, Ward Churchill, who would later, around the time that Joe became a famous blogger, gain infamy for using the phrase "little Eichmanns" to describe the World Trade Center workers who died on September 11. Back in Boulder, Churchill was a burgeoning activist for Indian country, and took Joe on numerous trips to reservations throughout the mountain West to meet warrior-intellectuals like Russell Means and Vine Deloria Jr. Joe was still a ceaseless reader, and would almost certainly have read Deloria's epochal *Custer Died for Your Sins: An Indian Manifesto*. Published in 1969, *Custer* was a wry and bitter essay collection about the historical exploitation of a rural minority—in many ways, a template for *Deer Hunting with Jesus*.

It was an era of agitation for Indian rights. In the summer of 1979, a federal court awarded the Sioux tribe more than $100 million in damages for their forced removal from Idaho's Black Hills region. The Sioux refused to take the money and began a prolonged, violent standoff. Joe patrolled the occupation's border with Ward Churchill and a group of John Birch Society members—imperfect but willing partners who had come on board out of shared contempt for the U.S. government. Two thousand miles from Highland Ridge, Joe had finally found a principled stand against the capitalist overthrow of rural folkways.

This was becoming a pattern. Despite his unbroken lifelong identification as a Virginia redneck, Joe seemed to always find his greatest common cause with people outside that mold, whether the upper-class gay friend who supplied his acid, the black coworkers he gained after Winchester businesses desegregated, or the minorities he encountered on trips through Central America, the delta South, and prairie West. He later became so well known for his dissection of rural white exploitation that his reputation overshadowed the real desires in his writing. He never pined for a return to backwoods white culture for its own sake; he wanted only community, connection, one-ness in the metaphysical and political sense, and he genuflected before any person or population that he felt understood those values, regardless of where they learned them. People who worked with their hands, who studied widely, who sought to open their third eye—anyone who rejected money as the be-all, end-all, and especially anyone who was exploited by profiteers.

And for all his obsession with Winchester, this value system came into sharpest focus during his time in Colorado. Self-fulfillment was the gospel of Boulder in the 1960s and 1970s, and Joe would look back on his time there as one of the happiest periods in his life: "All these years later I am beginning to understand the effect [that] living for a decade or so in a genuinely free time and place had on my life," he wrote in his *Deer Hunting* period, calling Boulder "paradise." But for all his expanded consciousness, after a decade in Colorado, Joe still hadn't managed to buy his family a house or develop a real career. Right before the dawn of the 1980s, right as Jeanne Mozier was opening up Berkeley Springs for East Coast hippie exploration, Joe made the agonizing decision to return home, to see if he could make a proper life in Winchester once more.

Joe had left town as a high school dropout, teen father, and purported drug casualty, but he returned as a seasoned journalist, and ended up working for the Byrds once again, this time on the staff of the *Winchester Star*. Remnants of the Granola Belt still clung to him: he kept twenty containers of vitamins in his office to advertise a strict regimen that he'd heard would give him total recall. But he also had a newfound confidence, even a swagger. He claimed a battered, dumpster-bound desk and high-backed chair for his office and wore a suit every day, fashioning himself a boisterous newspaperman. As editor of the local news section, he pushed his writers to dig more deeply into local political corruption. Needless to say, this did not enamor him to the Byrds, and neither did his push to unionize the newspaper staff. Virginia had a right-to-work statute in place since 1947 thanks in great part to Senator Harry Flood Byrd himself, and in any case the gospel of self-sufficiency made collective bargaining sound vaguely sinister, like something only Yankees and communists dared. The effort went nowhere.

It was 1979. The Apple Blossom Mall, the inland port, the factories—they were all still a few years away. But the failed unionization effort showed Joe that the bastards were still on the march and untouchable in Winchester. The town ran on money. People weren't looking for broadened horizons. And for someone with a bookshelf and a social conscience, there wasn't much solace to be found.

The only social comfort Joe had was a small group of guys who got together every few weeks to smoke pot and swim in the river, talking about books and politics. These were mostly outsiders, come-heres like the realtor Nick Smart, who sold Joe his first house. Nick grew up in Falls Church, Virginia, the heart of the D.C. suburbs, but left for Paris after college in 1959. He found his way to the Beat Hotel, where he lived on the same hall as Ginsberg and Burroughs. When he returned stateside, Nick married a younger girl from his hometown and, still flush with radical energy, set off for Paw Paw, West Virginia, where a rural commune was starting. For years, Nick and his wife were among the million-odd white Americans who went "back to the land" during the Vietnam era. Joe's experience in Boulder wasn't quite so rustic—no compost toilet or geodesic dome—but philosophically he was right in line with the readership of *The Foxfire Book*, *The Modern Utopian*, and *Mother Earth News*. He would eventually mourn how the media diminished the '60s as "a handful of newsreel snippets of the Haight Ashbury, Kent State, long hair, Vietnam and the Beatles." Joe knew the truth: a great portion of the counterculture lived among trees and wide skies, and he connected with Nick over their shared recognition of this.

Like many of their back-to-the-land peers, Nick and his wife returned to civilization when they had children and suddenly realized the limits of communard education. They moved to Winchester in 1974, when Nick became a realtor. By the time Nick met Joe, he was already familiar with the trade-offs that one makes in order to live in a place with good schools and pretty landscaping. He once asked a fellow businessman if he knew *The Great Gatsby*, and the man replied, "Is he from Frederick County?"

Nevertheless, Nick made his peace with the place, as so many come-heres would do over the following decades, including Barbara Dickinson and Matt Hahn. Relative to the D.C. region, Winchester was affordable, safe, and close to nature. Nick had a good public school for his girls and a growing market in which to learn the real estate trade. Joe had no such comforts; he knew the place too well. He saw its calmness as conformism, knew its natural scenery was shrinking and underappreciated. The *Star*, his only creative outlet, was a reactionary, right-wing, small-town paper owned by descendants of the man who made the Shenandoah synonymous with greed and small-mindedness. Plus, Joe had woes at home. He and Cindy separated in 1979, and Joe was devastated. He'd found his way into the Winchester middle class but didn't get any comfort from it. The divorce, as he surely recognized, would disrupt Timothy's life right at the age when Joe's had been shaken by the loss of Over Home. Adrift, he retreated to Colorado, the only place since where he felt that he truly belonged.

Trouble was, the forces of money and corporatization were bearing down on Boulder too. The city's conversion from hippie outpost to yuppie playground was well underway. The "People's Republic" vibe was losing out to higher costs of living and that perennial Virginia bugaboo, real estate development. The *Musical Express* was no more, though Joe managed freelance features with other local and national magazines. He also met a bright and idealistic woman named Nancy, who was writing a newsletter for the well-known Boulder Free School.

United in their disappointment over paradise lost, Joe and Nancy settled on a last-ditch response: in 1982, they got married and dropped out. Joe knew from his earlier travels that Indian land was cheap and set-apart, so they set out for the Coeur D'Alene reservation in the Idaho panhandle. But this was no longer the utopian moment that had attracted Nick and his wife and a million others. And anyway, most of those middle-class homesteaders a decade earlier had tried some kind of communal arrangement, whether sharing a house between multiple families or joining a collective like The Farm in Summertown, Tennessee. Joe and Nancy, by comparison, found a desolate, forest-adjacent plot about 10 miles from the nearest town, St. Maries. In case it wasn't clear enough that the peaceful '60s dream was over, their regional neighbors included Richard Butler's Aryan Nation compound.

The shack they bought had no electricity, running water, or address. It was located on a dirt road about halfway up a mountain, which must have recalled Shanghai Road. Joe worked tirelessly, clearing forest and planting a garden behind the house. He built a barn for horses and livestock, and tended bar at the reservation for spare cash. He had no time for writing, though he returned to painting, the hobby he'd had since childhood. He insisted on giving his work away for free to friends and visitors. Into this world of exile, art, and survivalist labor, Joe and Nancy's first child, Patrick, was born in November 1982. Their second, Elizabeth, arrived in May 1984.

To the extent that any couple can remove themselves from the politics and culture of a country while still living there, Joe and Nancy managed it, living more or less self-sufficiently other than rare trips to the St. Maries' food co-op. But as a quest for personal happiness it wasn't nearly so successful. The kids reached school age by 1988, and by that point the pressure of self-sufficiency had become unbearable. Like his father before him, Joe took his kids from the country to the city, in this case Moscow, Idaho, on the border with Washington. He and Nancy divorced soon after.

Having grown up in an unimaginably close-knit rural family and community, Joe was now forty-two years old with three children, two failed marriages, and no clear home. He took up writing again, this time for a local paper, the *Idahonian*, where he edited the Lifestyles section and wrote a regular first-person column. From his easy but musical style you wouldn't guess that he'd been chopping wood and tending to horses for the previous six years. He interviewed Woodstock attendees for the festival's twentieth anniversary, and touched on politics by talking to locals like "Big Leroy" about everything from gas prices to Vietnam veterans.

On January 23, 1990, Joe wrote an *Idahonian* column about Mississippi, particularly its blues traditions and poverty. The essay was wistful, even tender. After an evocative litany of southern scenery—kudzu, field hands, "bobbing white cotton"—he ended on a disarmingly vulnerable, not political, note: "I miss it. I really do."

Around this time he met Barbara, who was living in Pullman, Washington, right across the border. They were both stranded in rural college towns, but it turned out that she and Joe had more in common than isolation. For one, they were both divorced parents. And a decade earlier, Barbara had been an antiwar protester and vocal feminist in Madison, raising her son in a reflexively liberal community steeped in Gloria Steinem and *Free to Be You and Me*. From the first, she recognized a fellow traveler. Joe had no misogynist edge like many men of his era. Instead, they could talk about books and music. He cooked for her and reminisced about his own radical days, and slowly, hesitantly, they fell in love.

After getting married, Joe and Barbara pushed west. Eugene, Oregon, was a more liberal, cosmopolitan town than Moscow, but the move heralded the straightest, most middle-class period of Joe's life. He got a job for *Crop Production Management*, a glossy trade magazine that had one client, Conagra, which sent copies to its every customer. As editor, Joe was compelled to live the same impossibly lavish lifestyle as his publisher: dinners out on the corporate card, frequent jet trips to San Francisco, and expenses-paid vacations to Las Vegas with the wives where a $500 shopping allowance waited for them at check-in. Joe was suddenly a man for whom scotch preceded dinner, and dinner preceded brandy. Which is to say, he had finally caught up to the business class that ran Winchester, and to the kind of corporation, Conagra, that had driven the postwar Shanghai Road community into cities to be their subalterns.

And it made him miserable. He finally had money of his own, more than he'd ever expected to have, and came to the cliché realization that it didn't quiet his mind or offer any sense of meaning. And so he asked Barbara, what about Winchester? It was quiet and safe. They could be near family. With their savings and the lower cost of living, they could live right downtown, blocks from the beautiful, newly refurbished walking mall.

Their house was on the west side of town, far from the train tracks and closer to Washington Street, where JudySue had pointed out each wealthy family by name. With its pillars and spires, theirs fit right in, even if they had to clean a little black mold off the walls. The work kept Joe's hands busier than they'd been in years.

As promised, Barbara liked all the nearby woods and the broad sky. They made regular trips to the Blue Ridge and stared into the vastness that had entranced everyone from Alexander Spotswood to Jim McCoy. They took walks through every corner of downtown, and Joe had a story or a bit of gossip or a historical anecdote for them all. There were nights when the sunset was like a landscape painting. For a while, it appeared they'd made the transition from coastal middle-class boredom to something more rooted and fulfilling. Barbara even took a job doing genealogy research at the Handley Library.

Since Joe's last extended stay twenty years earlier, Winchester had become unrecognizable. There were new companies, and plenty of new monstrosities like Creekside Village. The Hispanic share of the population had nearly tripled, from just over 3 percent to more than 8 percent, many of whom worked in the apple industry. But a few things were familiar. His romantic memories were more painful at close range. He commuted every morning to his editing job at *Military History* magazine on the Harry F. Byrd Highway, and remembered just how permanent and indestructible the line had felt between his own family and the midcentury Winchester wealthy. More than 50 percent of Winchester residences were rentals, a fact Joe gleaned from conversations at working-class bars like the Royal Lunch, the Twilight Zone, and Coalie Harry's. He also learned that the biggest landlords served on the local government, and had efficiently excised any regulations for rental properties. The old anger returned, accompanied and amplified by the memory of his father trembling when the rent money ran out, and soon Joe founded the Winchester Tenant's Board.

He interviewed renters and gave away his own money when they needed it. He killed rats in the unregulated apartments and brought them to city council meetings in a cardboard box— anything to call attention to the abuse. While still commuting an hour each way during the week, Joe wrote regular scathing letters to the *Star*, detailing the exploitation. They published them, but nothing changed. So he ranted to Barbara, and to his bar mates. Soon the Twilight Zone could no longer contain his exasperation, and he began writing in chat rooms under the screen name "ScreamingMan." Then came "Howling in the Belly of the Confederacy," his first essay to be published online. It evoked a hellscape of contemporary southern deterioration: low-wage assembly-line jobs, rampant obesity, health-care price gouging, Limbaugh on a loop.

Similar tracts—about guns, alcohol, Pentecostalism, and other pillars of trailer-born Dixie living—appeared more frequently than most people exercise. His prose had always galloped, but now it became unstoppable. His essays were uniformly long-winded, comprising massive chunks of text that encompassed evocative memories, deep history, and present-day Winchester scenes. He was at the vanguard of political blogging, and his essays were published at some of the progressive left's more strident outposts, like EnergyGrid and CounterPunch. But Joe rarely wrote about the news. More often he wrote about anger, guilt, despair, drugs, and the lived experience of poverty and ill education. He rarely mentioned specific politicians, and when he did, he singled out corporatist democrats like Bill Clinton and John Kerry as often as he mentioned the then-current president.

This ornery, indefinable work proved relatable. Within months of his first publication, Joe was receiving so many fan e-mails that Ken Smith, a fan himself who had offered to create and manage joebageant.com, started running them on the site. They came from Fair Oaks, California, and Auburn, Washington; Du Quoin, Illinois, and Davenport, Iowa; Chatsworth Island, Australia; Leeds, Vancouver, Beijing. The writers tended to be Joe's age, with a similar perspective on America's fall. "My roots are in the Texas dirt, but I made a journey through the student radical acid communal left," said one. "Your articles remind me so much of my family. They are the same pissed off, ignorant white trash that fought their way from Virginia, through the Appalachians, to East Texas," said another.

As Joe's career took off, his rage became his brand. Reporters came to visit him and he put on a fishing vest and drove them up to the Royal Lunch and the Troubadour to show them how real folks lived. Joe garnered a reputation as a red-state Virgil, a guide to rural American disaffection writ large. In one photo essay from 2006, done in conjunction with a British photographer, he described Winchester by saying "This is my home. Home to everything thoughtless and dangerous about America these days, home to most of the people I have loved and certainly home to all my ghosts." After a tour through downtown, full of bile about the "Jim Crow apple," conservative Christianity, and the town's enduring Civil War preoccupation, Joe finally takes his guest up to the Troubadour, "one of the last tonk joints in our area. Suburbanization has driven them out. But the Troubadour still has a remote feel in that it is up on top of a mountain." Even in a short, tossed-off essay, his relief is palpable. "If you can't find hillbilly love here, honey, you're probably a Yankee."

Around this time, when the endless recording sessions for *Matt Hahn Sings the Songs of Jim McCoy* were underway, Joe was at work on his own demanding project. He signed his book deal in May 2005, making him the first person to jump from political blogging to mainstream publishing. The proposed title was *DRINK, PRAY, FIGHT, FUCK: Dispatches from America's Class Wars,* though late in the editorial process it was changed to avoid confusion with, of all things, *Eat Pray Love.*

The book was a minor sensation. Besides the blurbs from Zinn and Terkel, it caught the eye of Brad Pitt's production company, Plan B, which contacted Joe about doing a documentary series about Winchester. The project faltered, but the book still sold wildly in town. The Winchester Book Gallery, right on the walking mall, hosted the well-attended release party, though none of the town's upper crust dared attend. For weeks after, however, the same rich landowners that Joe had pilloried came in to buy three or four copies at a time to send to friends. The store's owner, a local many years younger than Joe, admired the writer's ability to appeal to wealthy vanity. "Maybe if Patsy had written a song about them, they would have left her alone," he said.

As more and more people read his writing and more journalists came to sit at his feet, Joe grew less and less hopeful that anything would change. He began looking away from his town, reaching out for grander truths. "It is seeing everything in material terms, just like our avaricious capitalist overlords, that holds us back," he wrote. "We are in the sixth great species die-off here."

In response, Joe used his book advance to move to Belize, a country he hadn't seen in thirty years, and then only as a tourist. As he told it, he arrived in country and soon met a young family from the town of Hopkins Village, a coastal outpost founded by the survivors of a slave ship crash. He agreed to fund and help build a guesthouse that the family could rent for extra income. As payment, he could stay in it for free whenever he came to Hopkins. Three thousand miles from Shanghai Road, Joe felt he'd found one last bastion of the communal, sustainable life that American consumerism had long since made impossible. "What I get out of it is a feeling of direct accomplishment that a man can never have in this country," he wrote on his site: "Being a working man in America means that, no matter how much you earn or how hard you work, it is never enough and the job is never done."

This was of course a little insincere. This proud third-world survivalist owned nice property in a historic district in Virginia. He paid taxes on it, or at least his increasingly suffering wife did; Joe wouldn't sully himself with such efforts. And while he was convinced of the impossibility of living a decent life in the contemporary United States, his old radical confreres had somehow managed. Jerry Roberts, who'd plastered Joe's early poetry around Boulder, was now the Boulder County assessor. And Nick Smart, late of the Beat Hotel and the Paw Paw commune, had moved from residential to commercial real estate—he had in fact sold the land to Walmart that allowed it to build its Winchester megastore. Nick was now living with his wife on an expansive country property right on the Shenandoah River, with his daughter and grandkids on the adjacent lot. In semiretirement, he was raising a few dozen head of beef cattle that he sold to butchers. He read all the same stuff that Joe read—fat books about inequality and elite malfeasance—and he wanted the same things that Joe wanted, namely a life of solitude on his own terms. But he'd somehow managed to bend his ideals just enough to play along with the system he despised. In his mind, bringing Walmart to Winchester was almost a Samson-like gesture of morally necessary destruction: Nick had no affection for the old-money business crowd, and at least the new corporate competition challenged their centuries-long hold on the region's every last dollar and civic decision. He and Joe still socialized and revered each other, but Nick was willing to make the normal compromises most people accept in order to buy affordable clothes or occasionally enjoy themselves in the first world.

Joe, by contrast, had become toxically pure. He wouldn't cede moral high ground to anyone. As a result, he also couldn't foster a true home or community, since coexisting with others requires sacrifice and compromise of a more mundane sort. He still lived half the year with Barbara in Winchester, but he joked that his months away were his gift to her. He knew he'd grown intolerably bleak, and he was so terrified of a third divorce that it seemed better to just stay away and avoid fights as often as possible. She didn't bother to discuss her own life because she didn't feel like getting a lecture or being made to feel petty. Compared with the Belizean poor, she had nothing to complain about, after all.

At the invitation of Ken Smith, Joe bought a cheap apartment in Ajijic, an expat-filled town near Guadalajara, Mexico. He needed a nearby international airport to make it to his frequent speaking invitations abroad. A few days before Christmas 2010, less than a week after Joe had gone into the Mexican mountains on horseback to drop acid with a group of gauchos, Ken took him to a doctor to have a nagging stomach pain checked out. An X-ray revealed a gastrointestinal stromal tumor, bigger in mass than his liver. It was clenched around his stomach like a fist, inoperable. "I don't want to die in the America I see emerging," he had written four years earlier, justifying his move to Belize. He would not get his wish. After three months in and out of VA hospitals and a prescription painkiller haze, Joe died with Barbara, Cindy, and his three kids by his side. In lieu of a funeral, they drove up to Shanghai Road and scattered his ashes in private. An outpouring of grief came on his website, where Ken rounded up dozens of tributes by bloggers and writers from around the globe. Joe was not memorialized in Winchester.

Given his nonstop battles with it before and after he returned as a well-off adult, the natural question is why Joe felt compelled to go back to Winchester in the first place. Perhaps he genuinely remembered it with affection, in spite of its flaws. Perhaps, like many displaced southern men on the far side of middle age, he simply missed the pace and climate. I suspect that he kept coming back throughout his life to prove he could beat the town—to show that he could transcend the role he'd been forced into as a child. But the shame of poverty still clung to him like rust. He could sense it in others, and couldn't forgive Winchester—or Virginia, or the United States, or the entire world—for making people live with it. The writing he did as an older man was his effort to burn it all to the ground. In *Deer Hunting with Jesus*, he wielded the full force of his self-education and counter-consciousness to fume at the people who profited off the land instead of honoring it. In *Rainbow Pie*, he valorized the people who had taught him to love the land in the first place. Neither effort bought him any goodwill locally. The rich folks were offended and the country folks didn't even read his books; they barely read at all. But in his small way, he laughed last. Anyone who reads these books will forget all about apples and Stonewall Jackson and artful latte foam. From now on, Winchester will be the American capital of small minds and venal cruelty.

I left the walking mall and drove back toward Berkeley Springs. Five minutes north of Winchester on Route 522, the highway becomes hilly and open, and begins to twist and roll. My favorite kind of road: a winding, two-lane, 50-mph state highway in the country. This is a commercially barren territory now, other than big signs advertising acreage. But I noticed a lone store on the southbound side, right in the notch of a mountain curve. There were no cars in the gravel lot when I rolled in and parked beneath a 20-foot-tall sign that read, in three faded yellow sections:

JOHN'S

MUSIC

GAS

Inside I found hundreds of square feet of shelf and table space, all piled high with cast-off knickknacks and domestic detritus. Praise it: a genuine redneck junk shop. Cowboy hats, Tasmanian devil T-shirts, themed salt and pepper shakers, bulbless desk lamps, shovels and hoes, stiff empty golf club bags, Christmas ornaments, nonfunctioning wall clocks, coasters, ashtrays, cloudy glass bottles, fishing rods, mugs with slogans like "WE CAN TALK ONCE I GET MY COFFEE!!!," dust-covered wicker baskets, and American flags, my god, so many American flags. All of it marked with tiny neon-orange price stickers, so if you squinted you saw only an undifferentiated brown mass of yard-sale garbage with an alien, orange-starred sky overlaid. The place reeked of mildew.

A sweaty, friendly man with big eyes approached and I learned that this was in fact John, who ran the store with his wife. Frankly, he looked like he needed a rest, and not only a few hours. With only the slightest provocation, he began an hour-long rant about the economy, though "began" probably isn't the word. From the sound of it, this was an ongoing inner sermon, and John spent his days tidying up his kingdom of unwanted gewgaws, waiting for someone to ask him about the state of the union.

"The people thought they were gettin' a bargain," he explained in a desiccated drawl. "They started sending their money to other states, other countries. I'm sorry, that's not a bargain. In this country, for a long while, you cannot run a legitimate business and get any farther than the end of the line. Everything now is trick-you this, trick-you that. Their business"—he pronounced it *bidness*—"is they leverage every point that they can. So until people educate themselves . . . they're not getting a bargain. Lotta times they're paying more. Walmart's the worst."

He kept going, directing his ire at the "bracket system," whereby a corporation sells its product in tiers—high-end, mid-price, and low-end, the last of which John's people are of course more than happy to buy. John's Music used to be a full grocery that fed every working person in a 20-mile radius, but he couldn't compete with a big chain's ability to buy in bulk, and he couldn't bring himself to stock the excitingly affordable half-filler meat that his neighbors fell in love with. More than anything, he sounded betrayed: his people fell for it. Lured by discounts, they hung him out to dry. After a few minutes of similar talk that could have been transcribed verbatim and passed off for a lost chapter of *Deer Hunting with Jesus*, I asked John if he'd ever read Joe Bageant.

"Never read his book, but I know him well," he said. "Joe brings his TV people in here, when they come to ask him about things. And those fishing vests. This right here is where he bought 'em."

I was disarmed by his use of the present tense. Uneasily, I asked if he knew Joe had died more than two years earlier. His shoulders sank.

"I . . . I had no idea," he said, wiping his forearm across his brow. He called over to his wife, who was sitting behind the register, near the glass jewelry case. "You know Joe Bageant died?"

"Joe Bageant?" she said. I watched a memory flood her face. "Oh no."

"How'd it happen?" asked John. I told him stomach cancer.

"Gosh." He took a long breath and stared out the window at the lonely highway. No one came in the shop.

"Joe, he was smart," John said finally. "He understood all this stuff. I can't believe this."

A huge part of Joe's appeal was his sympathetic depiction of people like John, and scenes like this rotting old knickknack graveyard. Joe knew that many liberals dismissed his people as heartless, dumb, or both. But he depicted them on their own terms. Without quite excusing the racist tendencies or religious zealotry in his community—and there were more than a few items in John's store to offend both the uptight and the faithless —he saw them as essentially victims. There were money-grubbing Republicans who gave empty lip service to their most conservative values, yes, but there were also supposedly enlightened liberals who overlooked rural white poverty because they dismissed those values out of hand.

The real message of *Deer Hunting with Jesus* was that rural poor people were in line to revolt before too long. Even lifelong hillbilly Democrats like those in rural Virginia could see that liberal politicians didn't have any interest in businesses that actually served as a locus for a community—places like the Troubadour. They could tell that raising a region's average household income isn't worth half a damn if it's achieved by installing hundreds of upper-middle-class families in prefabricated homes while those in trailers go into bankruptcy from their medical bills. Joe tried to warn his liberal readers that a reckoning was on its way. Lives were being destroyed out there in the heartland. Hard-working people were suffering unimaginably.

But his very insights and anger distanced him from the people he was advocating for. He was one of the last people in the

Virginias to grow up in a subsistence culture, and that culture's sudden end forced him to romanticize it beyond usefulness. He went from rural heaven to lower-class shame when he was only a child, and for the rest of his life he was unable to stick with any plan, place, or project for longer than about eight years. He burned through relationships, jobs, and residences with equal intensity, and was capable of leaving all of them without even a good-bye, just as he made his final exit without any public acknowledgment whatsoever. Something about the doomed transition from Over Home to Winchester inured him to upheaval and loss. He simply powered through life, forever the cornered animal, reading both success and failure as justification to escape elsewhere. After all, nothing lasts.

When the Internet finally presented Joe with a community of similar seekers, he responded generously. He brought his readers' voices onto his site and engaged them at length. He flew around the world to meet them in person. The response all over was the same as it was in John's junk shop: *Joe understands.* Despite multiple attempts, he never managed to create the kind of sanctuary that southerners value most—the place where neighbors and family can lay aside their troubles, like John's Music or Patsy's shift at Gaunt's or the Troubadour had all managed to be at one time. But he managed to express, with eloquence and tragic outrage, exactly why those kinds of places were now more endangered than ever.

Before leaving I picked out two records from John's massive selection of water-damaged LPs—an early Watson Family collection and a Carter Family album called *'Mid the Green Hills of Virginia,* complete with Shenandoah-looking cover art. John was still railing as his wife rang me up, and she shook her head and looked up at me over her glasses. It was neither a mocking look nor a complaining one, just a silent recognition: *Once you're gone, it's gonna be just me listening to this.*

The total came to $15, about five times what I would have expected for a couple pieces of warped vinyl. As I pulled out of the parking lot, John sat there, spilling out of his plastic lawn chair, sweating and sighing in a garage-door-shaped frame of afternoon Valley light. It might be hours until someone came in to buy something. Worse yet, it might be longer until someone came in willing to listen.

PART THREE

HOMEPLACE

7

———✦———

They'll Have to
Carry Me Out

THE TROUBADOUR WASN'T ONLY FOR parties.
The more I went, the earlier I tended to arrive, stopping at the
picnic tables before entering to enjoy a few minutes of daytime
cricket chatter or a stroll around the garden. Years after the fall of
the Highland Ridge canning industry, Jim's tomatoes still sprang
from the dirt like bamboo. The vines climbed hungrily and the
leaves gobbled sunlight. The late afternoon was the perfect time
to come here, to slow down and adjust to the mountain pace before the honky-tonkin' began. To hear the breeze rustle Jim and
Bertha's "hillbilly wind chimes," a quartet of crinkled Natural
Light cans hanging on string just outside their trailer door. To
see a squirrel scurry along the tall white fence, above the person-
alized canvas banner that Budweiser had sent for Jim's eighti-
eth birthday in 2009. And then, having gathered yourself and

let your city worries drift out into the air like Pall Mall smoke, to turn the doorknob and hear the way it squeaked, the way the door eased shut with a soft creaking groan. Early enough in the day, you could hear and feel just how many tired, relieved people had walked through that entryway and worn it down until it sighed just like they did.

On one such day, a TV had been set up by the stage, a first in all the times I'd been there. Codi was at the bar, dispensing long pours of rail liquor into a Sunny Delight bottle to make the night's Rocket Fuel. Bertha was counting receipts and talking idly to the sole customer, a big-bellied man in a tight T-shirt who sipped from a sweating bottle and picked at the paper label. Jim was sitting with a friend I didn't recognize, watching TV in silence. He gestured me over and I sat on his other side.

The program looked like a megachurch service: royal blue lighting, an ace backing band, impassioned speeches, wailing tears from the front row. Jim filled me in.

"George Jones's funeral," he said. "Charlie sent me up the tape from Nashville." We watched Mike Huckabee fawn. "He wanted me to come down for it." Jim's physical inability to make that trip hung in the air, unsaid.

Jones had died a few weeks earlier, after battling one of country music's most legendarily destructive relationships with alcohol. He lived into his early eighties and, despite lung trouble in his last years, was still performing in arenas less than three weeks before his death from respiratory failure. The funeral was held at the same Opry House stage that he'd lorded over for decades, as was only fitting: Jones and the Opry matured into institutions alongside each other, and pushed Nashville into its star-factory era, the Hollywood of the South.

Jones was born two years after Jim, and grew up similarly in a 2-square-mile town in east Texas called Colmesneil. He was musical from an early age, and entertained his large family by singing. Like Jim, he got his start playing on postwar country radio stations, and eventually found a home on Starday, one of the most successful of the honky-tonk-era record labels. He married young, had children young, and had his first chart success with bouncy pop country 45s like "Why Baby Why." This was the mode that Jim's Melody Playboys were versed in, but unlike Jim—unlike anybody—Jones had a voice that could blow down a barn. He sang the title syllables of "Why Baby Why" like a baritone siren; they sound authoritative no matter how small the speakers. He moved from Starday to Mercury Records in the late 1950s and found even greater fame, notably with "White Lightning," a believably nostalgic rocker about daddy's moonshine. Jones's career had its peaks and valleys through the 1960s, though industry respect for his voice only grew. But in 1969, soon after Jim McCoy had accepted fate and decided on a life in Winchester, Jones married fellow balladeer Tammy Wynette, and not long after that, moved to Epic Records and began working with producer Billy Sherrill.

Patsy Cline and Owen Bradley's innovation ten years earlier was to pull country out of the roadhouse and dress it in a tuxedo. They brought sophisticated, orchestral pop to the country charts, but Jones and Sherrill took the idea even further, situating the singer's voice amid swelling, precise arrangements that went for the emotional jugular. If Patsy's Bradley records invited the listener to sit down and share a slow drink, Jones's Sherrill records, like his signature song, "The Grand Tour," were almost built for Broadway. They were pure industrialized sadness, cruise missiles of heartbreak. Many of them were huge hits, especially his duets with Wynette, whom Sherrill also recorded solo. In 1974, the year of "The Grand Tour," the Grand Ole Opry moved from the Ryman Theater in downtown Nashville to a newly built megaplex about 10 miles outside town, later expanding it with a theme park and hotel. The genre's down-home days were dead and gone, and Jones and Sherrill had hastened their demise.

Though they triumphed commercially, even the titles of their songs are bleaker than Texas scrubland: "Things Have Gone to Pieces," "These Days (I Barely Get By)," "Ain't Nobody Gonna Miss Me," and my favorite, "I Just Don't Give a Damn." Jones had reason to pity himself: by the mid-1970s Wynette left him, and by the end of the decade he was homeless, malnourished, and increasingly known as "No-Show Jones" for his undependable attitude toward live performance. In 1979 he was committed to the Hillcrest Psychiatric Hospital in Birmingham, and upon leaving, immediately went to the store for beer. No country star had ever fallen farther and lived.

But live he did, and in 1980 Jones met with Sherrill in Nashville to record yet another epic tearjerker, "He Stopped Loving Her Today." Jones famously despised the song, yet sang it with studied, stunning emotional control, opening almost conversationally and climaxing like a country Caruso. The song was a hit, a huge one, but the effect of "He Stopped Loving Her Today" can't be measured in radio play or records sold. The song redefined how country sounded. It inaugurated the genre for the 1980s, with diamond guitar arpeggios and upwardly spiraling string flourishes: tear-in-your-beer for the era of *Star Wars* and hair metal. The song somehow did this without diminishing Jones as an artist; it was the rare blockbuster that seemed personal and pained. It bought him immortality. George Jones ascended to heaven while still alive.

This explained the overwhelming tone of the memorial service, which, besides Huckabee, included remarks from former first lady Laura Bush and a procession of tearful tributes from younger stars. Vince Gill nearly collapsed sobbing while singing "Go Rest High on That Mountain," until Garth Brooks led a standing ovation to support him through. Throughout, Jones's widow—Nancy Sepulvado, his fourth wife—sat in the front row, convulsing with sadness. This truly was the world that Jones and Sherrill wrought. Music had always been the only setting where country-bred white people allowed themselves to be beset by their emotions, but those weapons-grade weepers of the 1970s and '80s delivered the atomic era of country bombast and piety. No one could be expected to hold back with George Jones's casket in view.

Nevertheless, Jim managed. As Alan Jackson closed the show with a stoic version of "He Stopped Loving Her Today," Jim watched stone-faced.

"Vince Gill's a good one," he said. That was how he spoke of any country music after 1980—singers were either good or they got an eye-roll. And "good" basically meant they paid adequate tribute to the postwar years. Jim's taste froze in amber right around the time that Billy Sherrill appeared on the charts. At that point, music became just the biggest of Jim's many means of getting by.

Jim opened a convenience store, the Real McCoy, selling beer and cold cuts and chips in downtown Winchester. He kept the record shop down in Ward Plaza on the town's southwestern edge, and regularly set up a band on a flatbed truck in the parking lot to attract customers. Ever the cross-marketer, he gave record store coupons to his convenience store customers and vice versa. He coordinated bus tours to Nashville for Shenandoans who wanted a pilgrimage to the Opry. He remained a DJ, of course, and produced records while maintaining a steady schedule of live gigs. By the early 1970s, he was still locally famous enough that people would come in the record store to sell him songs they'd written.

That's how he met Bertha. She grew up in a tiny town called Romney, West Virginia, on the south fork of the Potomac between Blues Beach and Pancake. Fifteen years younger than Jim, she came in one day in 1970 with wild curly blonde hair and claimed to be a songwriter. Her favorite act? Who else—George Jones. She couldn't sing but she could strum and hum well enough. And while nothing ever came of her songs, she kept returning to the store. She offered to watch Jim's little twins, Penny and Angel, now nearly ten, while he worked and kept his small empire running. Unlike the two ex–Mrs. McCoys, Bertha loved country music and respected the idea of a musician. She had children of her own, two boys and a girl from an earlier marriage that had soured even worse than Jim's own attempts. Her kids were shuffling between family and foster homes while Bertha scrambled to accumulate the minimum dollar amount needed for basic dignity in the United States. Jim, despite his own seven children, must have seemed like a good influence in that effort. He was older and owned a few businesses. He was known—by name, voice, and reputation. When you came from little hidden places like Berkeley Springs or Romney, those were the things that made a man. Bertha didn't care that Jim never had a hit record; he'd made it to the vicinity of actual stardom with nothing but pluck and hard work. He'd come from the mountains and made his way into the music industry. People relied on him and trusted him. And he could croon a little, as his late-'60s single "This Heart" made clear. He sold it in his stores and got it played on the radio, but it went nowhere. That didn't matter to Bertha. Jim had been everywhere.

His most consistent destination in those days was the *Wheeling Jamboree*, named for the host city in the northern panhandle of West Virginia. Home to steel companies, Interstate 70, and a Catholic university, Wheeling was a market town not unlike Winchester — the first major trading post west of Pittsburgh. Aspirationally dubbed "the Opry of the North," the *Jamboree* did draw quite a crowd every week (including my own father, who was a heavily bearded Neil Young acolyte and a member of Wheeling College's class of 1974), so Jim made the trek many times. These gigs brought union scale, $11 a show, so he usually picked up an additional late-night bar set in town as well. The drives out west and back were a challenge. The rocky, swooping Alleghenies made the Blue Ridge seem positively tender, and the sky above Wheeling was more steely and angry than the wide-open vistas around Highland Ridge. The northern panhandle winter, too, could be a slushy, windy ordeal, and the interstate meant sharing the road with 18-wheelers. But the *Jamboree* offered time on radio and television, and crucial networking with artists who sometimes came to record at Jim's home studio, Sounds of Winchester.

Bertha watched the girls and soon became an everyday part of their lives. Eventually they asked her, "Can we call you mom?" When she looked at them she thought: Penny and Angel, a coin and the heavens, commerce and the cosmos, identical twins. It really did sum up how Jim saw the world. He sought out the places where the road met the sky, and he knew they were everywhere around us. It was possible to find paradise on earth. You can live in Hillbilly Heaven.

A portrait of them from the time shows Jim with live-wire

curly hair of his own, balancing Bertha on his knee as they both laugh gleefully, mouths agog. Jim was heavy then, thick around the belly and a little puffy-faced, like the rest of his body had finally caught up with his eyes. But that was the truth: he was more himself in those days than in years past, better aligned. The businesses, the family, and the music were all in balance, or at least heading there. He was still traveling constantly, but covering less distance and returning to the same places more frequently. As much it could for someone with his boundless energy, his world had narrowed to something like routine.

The shattering came in 1977, when his son Andrew, from his first marriage, was found dead. It looked like drugs, though Jim, who never dared to walk that path himself, had a hard time accepting it. He persisted for decades in saying that Andrew had an accident. The boy was only in his mid-twenties. Not quite fifteen years after losing Patsy, Jim returned to Shenandoah Memorial Park and stood over an even more painful grave site as the dirt rained down by the shovelful. Like so many country people, he knew the realities of country songwriting intimately: no stability is permanent, no peace is beyond tragedy's reach.

In 1978, right as George Jones was headed for rock bottom and Joe Bageant was reaching his own wits' end in Boulder, Jim married his Romney gal and settled down even further. He took an interest in gospel and religious music—music he'd known as a child but had naturally drifted from over those decades in highway bars. He started recording some of the vocal groups from Winchester's black churches, and became manager of Winchester's gospel radio station, WEFG, whose call letters stood for "Where Everybody Finds God." He opened a 1-800 number called the Heavenly Hotline, staffed by prayerful neighbors all hours of the day and night. From 11 p.m. to midnight, seven nights a week, Jim hosted the *Heavenly Hotline* call-in show, featuring guest preachers and ministers from throughout the Virginias. He helped talk more than a few men down from suicide, live on-air. Those truckers from the Winchester–Wheeling route were frequent callers, lonely men on the ropes. It was like country music without the instruments—desperate people reckoning with life's deepest pain and entertainers offering salvation through the indisputable truths. How many men like Joe Bageant's father were forced off the land to drive corporate goods along the nation's ugliest roads? How many others were driving unsafely for hours, days on end, without even the promise of a paying audience on the other end? These were Jim's people, the men who had made that journey from mountaintop living to city labor, and knew the troubles that it brought. Those troubles were not getting any easier in the late '70s, and they wouldn't for a long time, as Joe Bageant or old junk-shop owner John would later realize. Jim recognized that this specific kind of rural heartbreak was becoming so common that only Jesus could help. Eventually he recorded *Jim McCoy Touches Your Heart*, a spoken-word album of stories and Bible verses that, like all the records he produced at the time, appeared on eight-track cassettes that he and Bertha copied and shrink-wrapped in their own home. His supply of blank tapes came from his friends at Starday Records.

In 1980, the year of "He Stopped Loving Her Today," WEFG switched to rock music, and the market for Jim's sacred work suddenly disappeared. He was forced, in his words, to "backslide." Back to country radio, to hits and ad-reads and no talk of saving souls. Back full-time to beer and cold cuts and selling other people's records. The dawn of a new decade meant Jim was now in his fifties, the age when most people start thinking about "home" in a different way. Especially people like Jim, who'd known a home that was so thoroughly set apart, so purposeful and well established. He journeyed back up to Highland Ridge, which by this point was a grown-over plot of brambles surrounding the vacant McCoy homestead. Still: that view. That air. So far from the dire backroad drives and the insatiable schedules of retail and radio. Like Joe Bageant, like Jeanne Mozier, like Julian Wood Glass Jr., Jim McCoy went to his partner and said: time to head for the country.

I left Jim to the TV as he got up to rewind the George Jones tape. Back at the bar, Codi was wiping down the counter.

"He's been watching that video for two weeks straight," she said. "Plays it for everyone who comes in."

Bertha was resting in her usual spot, the table right by the entranceway where she and Jim held court all night. I sat down and she looked at me with those weary eyes that always seemed to ask, *How much longer do I need to do this?* I asked her what it was like to come up here in the mid-'80s.

"Wasn't nothing here. I hated it."

Then why come?

She looked over her shoulder at Jim, watching the memorial all over again in his baseball hat and flannel shirt.

"He always gets what he wants."

The room around us was proof of that. Bertha was idolized —present in many of the pictures, her name on the signage— but without a doubt the shape and character of the Troubadour were completely defined by Jim. This was another way in which he and George Jones were formed by the same universe: country music is a patriarchy. Mothers are deified, but fathers are the unquestioned rulers. No chance that a female singer would have been allowed to debase herself with alcohol the way that Jones did, or that she'd be forgiven and welcomed back to the charts afterward. Jim never tried anyone's patience in this way, but once he'd established himself as king of a certain sliver of his world, the shots were his to call. No matter what kind of change it would be for Bertha or the kids, they went where Jim wanted.

"They had to clear it all, and even burn down the old house," Bertha explained. "He stood on the hill watching and told me, 'They started the fire in my bedroom.'"

They had 4 acres up there. Jim sold 2, then set up the trailer and planted the garden. He was content. He appreciated the full-circle quality of it all, and was happy to be living slowly again. He told Bertha that he would die up here. "They'll have to carry me out," he said.

They had no intention of hosting musicians all the way up on the roof of the world, but the phone kept ringing and friends kept asking the same question: Where are we going to play? Jim had left a hole in Winchester. The country regard for patriarchs isn't put-on—people were ready to follow him. It started with parties on the fresh grass outside. A few grills. Then before long, Jim, who was still commuting regularly down the mountain to spin records on the radio, couldn't keep from scheming.

There was space enough for a stage or more. He could see it, could feel the old entrepreneurial tingle coming back. He called on friends to help him gather the bricks and the lumber and he got to work. The only obstacle was family. Down the road, Jim's younger sister Faye was an active presence at a Highland Ridge church, and got wind that Jim had a mind to turn the homeplace into one of his temples of beer and sin. She came by the property to keep an eye on his construction, then she enlisted her parishioners in a petition against the place. Jim needed a cover. So he built something quicker, nearer to the road: another grocery

store. They had racks and shelving left over from the Real Mc-
Coy, and soon Jim was the neighborhood source for milk and
bread and other things. Behind the register, out of Faye's judg-
mental sight, the hammers kept flying and the sawdust spiraled
into the air.

It all came together naturally over time, like the land yearned
for it. A trailer, a garden, a store, a stage. By 1986 or '87—neither
Jim nor Bertha could quite remember; it was all joyous, constant
work without a real finish line—there was a functioning venue.
They never advertised or received any coverage in the *Morgan Messenger,* the newspaper with offices right on Washington
Street in Berkeley Springs. It was all friends, people who knew
that a party with Jim and Bertha justified itself. True word-of-
mouth expansion. Before long they had employees, and neighbors and friends who could benefit from an occasional fund-
raiser concert. He had recording equipment, so eventually he put
the trailer out back and kept that business going as well. In 1993,
recognizing a need and potential revenue source, he added another trailer, the West Virginia Country Music Hall of Fame.

Neighbors and tourists began to depend on Jim and Bertha's
new ramshackle compound. Without even meaning to, they'd
created an institution. Friday and Saturday nights especially, it
became hard to find a seat. In the early years there would be
fights, beer-empowered macho stuff that Jim had to settle down
and occasionally ban people for. Some folks ended up sleeping
in their cars, or more accurately, passing out while attempting to
drive home. The cops almost never came up the mountain roads,
so more than a few other visitors made wobbly, squinting midnight drives back. Eventually, even Faye arrived. Weekend nights
she sat near the stage, tapping her toes as one of Jim's friends
and acolytes played a version of the music she'd heard from the

battery-powered Victrola on this same ground, many long years earlier.

People would say that the Troubadour, as Jim eventually named it, was a last vestige of all the gone-away highway spots that his generation had known so well. But its roots were deeper than that. It was a bastion of an older type, a remnant of that lost epoch where people "made their own world with their own hands," as Joe Bageant wrote of his grandparents in *Rainbow Pie*. The Troubadour's isolation became its reason for being. Jim and Bertha's entire acreage was solely devoted to the only work that's really worth anything in this world: giving people a place to feel themselves.

With his tape of the Jones funeral still playing for no one, Jim took a seat near me at the far end of the bar, a rare sight. He kept pulling on his cigarette as I asked him if he remembered Joe Bageant. He briefly smiled.

"Oh, I remember Joe. Always bringing them TV people up here. Liked to have a few beers." Codi walked over and delivered a check to the only other customer. He reached into the back pocket of his jeans and pulled out a black leather wallet, counting out the price of a dozen wings and untold drinks in ones and fives.

"The thing about Joe was," Jim continued, unprompted, "he understood all this." He attempted to wave his cigarette hand to indicate the whole interior of the bar, but it only shook a little and hung in the air. I looked around the Troubadour's glowing, shabby splendor. I noticed for the first time that there was a web of dollar bills taped to the drop ceiling around the fan above the bar. I asked him to explain what exactly Joe understood.

"All of it." This time he didn't bother gesturing, he just inhaled more smoke. Jim wasn't saying that Joe knew the bar, he

187

was saying that Joe knew everything the bar stood for. What it symbolized. He understood the specific way that life gnaws and tears at rural people, the way their bodies and their homes come to wear the scars of their struggles. That mixture of unhealthy food, desperate payday partying, ceaseless labor, and outdoor worry takes a toll. The men often end up looking like Jim did with Bertha on his knee: overweight, overworked, sunburned, and overly fond of alcohol, but also defiantly joyful.

Codi brought change to the man in the T-shirt.

"Time to get home," he said, and handed back a few of the bills. "How about one more Wild Turkey?" She poured him a shot and he held the glass up toward me and Jim.

"One more for the road," he toasted. "In case we die."

Later that evening I came down Johnson's Mill Road myself, pausing at the intersection with Washington Street in downtown Berkeley Springs. There was a gas station to my left, which doubled as the welcome sign for anyone coming off the mountain to rejoin civilization. Across the street was the town's hippie-styled restaurant, specializing in veggie wraps and barbecue ribs. To the right of its brown facade, a narrow, nondescript driveway entrance fell off out of view. I'd never even noticed it before, but now, right at the cusp of sundown, I could see that a hazy light was shining in the distance, back farther than I would've thought that driveway could go. I drove across the street and entered.

The narrow road opened into a series of small parking lots that led up to a wide white steel barn. That's where the light was coming from: two flood lamps beamed above the tall doors and some vividly well-lit party was underway inside. I parked amid huge pickup trucks and dented sedans and joined a loose flow of multigenerational families toward the yellow-white glow.

A huge sign on the white hangar advertised that this was the Berkeley Springs Sportatorium, and the occasion was an amateur wrestling event: Hot & Bothered, a production of Covey Promotions. Two enormous men, some of the tallest and heaviest-looking human beings I'd ever seen, stood in dark sunglasses and sleeveless T-shirts along the gravel path leading up to the doors. They checked all bags and watched the procession skeptically: bouncing little kids with their parents, preadolescent boys with their friends and one tired mother trailing far behind, couples with their hands in each other's rear jean pockets, all the way up to grannies with walkers and even an old man on a scooter with an oxygen tube in his nose.

Passing in the shadow of our silent, skyscraping security pair, I found myself within earshot of a particularly awkward trio: another prepubescent boy with poor posture, his mother, and her overeager date. The boy was small and nearly frail in a polo shirt and buzz cut, the man was tall and Sears-catalog handsome, and the woman stood between them, trying for balance.

"This'll be great," the man said. "You excited, Corey?" The boy stared straight ahead and said nothing.

I stayed near them as we entered and paid our $15 per person and took our seats by the ring. To the left, a store-bought multicolored disco light rotated above a black curtain. To the right, two women at a table with chips and soda were doing fleet business. The elderly folks all sat in the front row while the younger kids ran around on Mountain Dew fumes. I looked at the program, an ink-jet printout listing the night's bouts. There would be the Tag Team Title Match between the duos Good Vibes and Double Dragon, a Television Title Match between a cop-styled character named John Boy Justice and a businessman known as The CEO. These and other costumed men were posed fearsomely on the flier, leering, posing, and pixelated in a crude collage. I recognized a few by the snack table, the Good Vibes pair, who wore pastel-colored zebra-stripe pants and spandex tops and were built like medium- and large-size barrels. Their fans gathered for pictures as the Vibes flexed muscles and held up number-1 fingers.

"Corey's been looking forward to this all week," his mother explained to Mr. Sears, who was dressed in a starched plaid button-down shirt and khaki slacks so sharply creased he could have used them to shave. The mother turned to the boy.

"Did you thank Luke for taking us here?" Corey was unmoved.

"My pleasure," said Luke. "Never been to one of these. Looking forward to it." An unbearable silence passed as Luke looked pleadingly at his girlfriend. She took mercy on him.

"You want to go get an autograph?" she asked her son, digging in her purse for a pen. She handed him one and pressed the program into his hands. He looked hesitant to leave her side but she nudged him gently, confidently, and he sidled past me and on toward the mugging mammoths in spandex. Luke pulled his hand through his hair and sighed. No man with a belt-clipped phone had ever looked more vexed.

"I just don't know," he said. "He's not talking. I'm . . . I'm trying here."

"You worry too much," she assured him. "He's fine. He likes you." Luke was so unconvinced he laughed. She amended her statement. "He's happy to be here."

Over on the other side of the crowd, Corey stood between the twin towers of Good Vibes as someone clicked a photo on a phone, then as he started to walk back toward us, a man took hold of a microphone in the middle of the ring. The music hushed—it had been chugging, maximal-energy hard rock ever since we walked in—and he leapt into an emcee routine that was calibrated a few notches beyond what the scene required. To this audience of country families amid bright lighting and bulk snacks, he brought a galloping cadence clearly meant for TV, not unlike the practiced patter between Arthur von Wiesenberger and Jill Klein Rone, which I'd watched only a hundred or so yards up the road.

"Hello, Berkeley Springs!" he shouted. "We want you to be loud and boisterous, we want you to cheer for your favorites. We want you to boo for your un-favorites." He then led the crowd in a call-and-response of cheering and booing, getting everyone accustomed to the shouting required for broadcast. Two cameramen were roving around the ring, preparing to start the live feed on the local cable-access station, footage from which would later be repurposed for the weekly hour-long Covey Pro highlight reel on the same channel. These broadcasts, which were also archived to YouTube, contained advertisements for bail bonds, local lawyers, and Berkeley Springs restaurants.

"But first let's rise and gentlemen, please remove your caps." A recorded, melismatic version of "The Star-Spangled Banner" played over the loudspeakers as crowd members shushed their kids and held their hands above their hearts.

"How's that autograph?" Luke tried once the recording ended, and Corey passed him the program. "Got 'em both? That's cool." Corey held close to his mom as our emcee introduced a minister, a tall man clad mostly in black who spoke in a similarly television-friendly way.

"Friends, we just celebrated the seventieth anniversary of D-day, so I would like, if any veterans are here with us, would you please stand and be recognized?" A few younger men and our oxygen-dependent neighbor rose from their chairs and received their due reverence. The preacher started back in.

"Dear Lord, we are truly here in the land of the brave and the home of the free. Thanks to these brave men and women who have defended our constitution and sacrificed for our freedom. But we thank you for your greater sacrifice, of your son. May we have a great show, keep everybody safe, and in all these things we give you the glory." A mumbled "amen" lifted out of the crowd.

"Thank you," said our emcee, retaking the mic. "One last reminder, folks, there is no smoking except on the gravel outside. If you are not standing on gravel, please keep from smoking." This was in keeping with local smoking laws, which even in rural West Virginia had grown prescriptive to a degree that would have been unimaginable even ten years earlier. Morgan County passed its ban on smoking in restaurants in 2007. The ban did exempt bars, however, meaning that Jim and Bertha had to legally classify their venue as such, since a smoking ban in a honky-tonk would be an affront to country living. But that meant that no kids were allowed in the place anymore, at least not indoors.

Strange as it may sound, the Troubadour used to resemble this wholesome family scene prior to that. In communities where there's not much going on, the distinction between a family venue and a grown-up one tends to blur. A single bar can be the place where one man brings his kids for payday dinner and another man finds the night's romance. Children in these settings are exposed to the whole messy tumble of adult life from an early age. Anita, who I'd met in the Half Note Lounge, recalled seeing Patsy Cline with her aunt and uncle at the kinds of places that Winchester's elite were decrying as indecent. For years it went unchallenged that the members of a community should be able to smoke in the same place where they entertained their children. That changed in the early twenty-first century, and it might seem like a small thing except for the fact that it deprived children of those wondrous, aesthetically edifying interiors that define the country mind. The Troubadour could provide a preadolescent with a window into the full range of human feeling, smells, and humor, bathed in deep Christmas red. It could mark a person's values for life.

His night may have been smoke-free, but Corey was certainly getting a fair taste of this humid, high-intensity southern humanity at Hot & Bothered. The high ceilings and metal walls of the Sportatorium made the place echo with boos and hurrahs. The sun was going down outside but it wasn't getting any cooler. The mosquitoes gathered and spun around the lights by the doorway. The stale air took on the smell of sweat and powdered cheese. Dots and circles formed in Luke's armpits and back, darkening his blue button-down shirt as he sat with his elbows on his knees, his hands connected only at his fingertips like a church spire. Corey hung close to his mother, scanning the room, quietly absorbing a southern community through sensory overload and trying to make sense of the physically and emotionally outsize adult world. Right on cue, the wrestlers entered the ring.

Hulks all, but none exactly muscular. More like bomb-shaped, thick, human punching bags built for bludgeoning and bruising. Good Vibes were up against Double Dragon in the tag-team round. Double Dragon were two white guys with black hair dressed in matching black-and-orange singlets with Chinese dragons crawling up their legs. Their bout was a brutal slap-stick ballet. The men scaled the ropes and flew face-first into the hard canvas, they threw themselves backward to amplify the effects of a forearm to the face. Elbows and heels flew at close range, and each of the four men got his turn to be choked between an opponent's armpit and elbow notch. Whoever wasn't fighting stood high on the corner ropes, compelling the crowd to wilder screams. They needed little encouragement. Finally, in a whirlwind of spins and collisions and suffocating holds, Double Dragon were disqualified for unsportsmanlike conduct: using a chair. The bruisers of Good Vibes had their bulky arms held high, and emerged from the ring with a pair of hand-painted championship belts that they draped on their shoulders. The cameras snapped around them as they held shaky number-1 fingers up, still sucking air.

The other matches followed the same template of crushing limbs and audience-minded peacocking, but the characters were like something from a semiotician's dream. First came the match between John Boy Justice, a mustachioed policeman, and Charles Everett Osgood, aka The CEO, who entered in a suit jacket that had been painted with a dollar sign across the back. The cop beat back the moneyed man with a baton, a symbolic battle that obviously meant more to the crowd than surfers and martial artists. The boos against The CEO grew deafening as he traipsed by the ropes, holding a hand to his ear and laughing smugly. Here was a heel worthy of rural America.

"They really hate him, don't they?" asked Luke, as Corey avoided making eye contact with him. "So do I. Who do you want to win, Corey?" the man asked, soldiering onward.

Summoning impressive courage, the boy looked over at the interloper and replied, "I like The CEO."

"Really?" Luke asked. "Okay, well that's who I'm rooting for too I guess."

The cop baton-bashed the businessman once again, then pounced, holding him to the floor as the referee slid around on his stomach with a whistle in his mouth.

"He's got him! He's got him!" yelled the ringside emcee. The audience's howl was like an arena-size answer to the noise that the Troubadour's karaoke night crowd made as Gay sang the opening bars of "Crazy."

The next two matches were even more crudely crowd-pleasing. First, Aken Pembrooke, a self-styled preppie with a cardigan tied loosely around his neck, fought Big John Greene, a sullen farmhand in green overalls. Pembrooke's beard was perfectly trimmed, Greene was neatly shaved. Pembrooke looked barely out of college himself, Greene looked positively aged. It occurred to me that Greene wasn't even a character—like an actual farmer, his movements were efficient and never oversold. The two men came together and locked hands at the head. They scuffled and threw each other down. Big John Greene earned the crowd's adoration purely by being there, dressed and named like that. Pembrooke stalked and strutted, teasing him and luxuriating in boos.

Finally Pembrooke had him on his back, straining as the farmer's bulk twisted and flexed beneath him. Pembrooke popped up to summon more hatred once the whistle sounded, but Big John Greene just pulled himself up one knee at a time, as unemotive as when he entered. They cheered him as he left the ring, another day's work done.

Before the class-struggle lessons of that bout had even been absorbed, another eminently despicable archetype sauntered onto the canvas: Louis B. Rich, a cigar in his mouth and a stack of fake bills in his hand. He counted a few off and threw them to the crowd. Children ran for the papers as they fluttered on the way down. The man with the oxygen tank held up two thumbs-down and shook his head in disgust.

Then a human bolt of lightning ran into the ring. A stringy, almost ferretlike creature in a trucker's hat and long cargo pants, he entered shirtless and scaled the ropes to beat his chest. He leaned forward toward the crowd and stuck out a massive tongue which had been stained a deep, unnatural blue, like he'd just chugged a handle of antifreeze. This feral redneck madman was fan-favorite Crazii Shea, who everyone around me seemed to know and adore. He was a harder archetype to identify. He looked like something Big John Greene had caught in the hills and raised against the odds, keeping him fenced at night and throwing him occasional pork trimmings. Shea ran around Louis B. Rich like a dervish, flailing and slobbering. He summoned rabid love from the crowd, even Corey, who no longer felt the need to be iconoclastic. He finally smiled and hooted like a little kid, and the relief in his mother's face was tremendous.

The bell rang. Crazii Shea spun and spit and flung himself at his opponent, who responded with calm but authoritative deflections and stomps. Trapped in a headlock, Shea let his blue tongue bulge out while his rangy arms and legs danced madly. He threw the wealthy bastard against the ropes and pounded his face when he sprang back. Rich grabbed Shea in midrun and twirled him up into the air before slamming him to the ground. When Shea landed on the mat, he sprang up in an instant and ran back for more. Eventually his energy began to work against him. He wobbled, woozy with exhaustion, and Rich tossed and punched him at will, throwing his body to the mat like a butcher slapping steak across the chopping block. His back and shoulders were raw from the canvas and ropes, and small red ribbons shone on his knuckles where the skin had broken. Shea's tongue displays, once meant to scare, were now the best he could do. He stuck his tongue out to prove that he was still wilder than Louis B. Rich, even in defeat. He was his own man. Money could beat him, but he would not be tamed or impressed by it.

Finally the wealthy villain held Shea's back to the mat. His legs twisted and turned like a fox fighting against a constricting snake, and at least one child screamed, "No, Shea!" as the referee raised a palm and slapped it down like the hand of fate. Corey fell back to his seat.

Shea was still a god after his loss. Corey stood in line behind a dozen others, and when his time came, the madman put his hand on the boy's shoulder and held his tongue out. Luke watched, itchy from the heat, while Corey's mom clicked her smartphone camera and immortalized the boy's hard-won Friday night joy. A pummeling, heavy rock song blared on the speakers indiscernibly, bouncing off the white corrugated metal walls and echoing out into the quiet blue hills.

Corey had learned some time-honored lessons in that sweltering gymnasium, ones that previous generations of small-town boys had learned from George Jones records—about the persistence of heartbreak, the challenges of family, the endless threat of men with money and power. In his small town's only Saturday entertainment, where prayers were offered for soldiers before the crudest urges were satisfied by showmen, Corey had witnessed a twenty-first-century version of a long-running American notion of communal escape: the revival tent, the traveling circus, the barn dance, movie house, or honky-tonk.

Throughout 2015, the rowdy nights got further and further apart up on Highland Ridge. I came up on a couple nights during winter and saw only a few cars in the lot, their exhaust fumes curling into the freezing, neon-hued air like dragon's breath. When the weather warmed up the numbers barely changed, until finally the time came one June Saturday when I parked at 7 p.m. and saw only a couple motorcycles parked outside. Though the quiet months and Jim and Bertha's perpetually failing health had prepared me, I still winced at the small sign that had appeared by the entrance door: FOR SALE.

Bertha was at the bar, talking to the two Harley couples and apologizing for the lack of tap beer. A NASCAR race was playing on the TV above the empty salad bar, soft enough that I could hear the bikers grumble as they popped open their Coors Light cans.

"Nope, no band tonight," said Bertha, waving to me.

The unamused bikers sipped their cans, tipped lightly, and ambled back to the parking lot to figure out which mountain switchback to go roaring through. Then Bertha looked over to me and said, with impatience: "He's out back if you wanna visit him."

Outside it was early twilight, and I saw that the picnic tables in the park had been turned into makeshift commercial displays. There were rows of VHS tapes, scratched-up plastic cups and plates, silverware, toolkits, kids' toys and bikes, faded Disney paraphernalia. All sitting in the shade, priced to go, waiting for someone to offer them a second or third life. Long ago, walking through John's Music, I'd wondered how these kinds of redneck junk shops come to be. Now I understood. No one sets out to own a place like this.

I'd never been in Jim's actual home, the trailer he shared with his wife. It was right there, next to the parking lot for all to see, but it was the one portion of the Troubadour grounds that wasn't open for business. I walked over, past the little white fence and through the short yard filled with plastic lawn ornaments, ascended two steps, and knocked on the trailer door. I didn't wait for him to answer before I poked in.

It was dim and overstuffed like every surface of Jim's life. Recording equipment by the coffeemaker, phone books piled on a fabric recliner. Hundreds of loose pages stood in sloping piles on a plastic card table by the door, mostly printed-out comments from the Troubadour Facebook page. A monitor by the window showed the security-camera footage from the parking lot. Jim was on the couch, trucker hat on, gazing up at a TV playing Fox News. I'd never heard him speak a word about politics. He lowered the volume as I sat down next to him on the couch.

"This used to be my office," he said apologetically. "It's a rehab place now. They wanted me close by the bar so they could keep an eye on me. Keep me outta trouble."

He'd been in the hospital six times in the previous seventeen months, for three separate operations. He hadn't been in the bar in weeks, hadn't had a drink in over a year. As for cigarettes, he was trying to quit. Matt Hahn and Jim's team of doctors down at Winchester Medical Center had him on some pills that made tobacco taste terrible, but sometimes he just needed to smoke to calm his frustrations. Cigarettes helped soothe him as he sat holed up in his living room, unable to run around tending to all the things that needed his attention. He pulled one out, lit it, drew in deeply, and tossed the pack on the couch.

"You wanna feel something?" he asked, and pulled my hand over to his midsection. Underneath the work shirt I felt something that I probably wouldn't have guessed was a human body if

I'd had my eyes closed. More like scrap wood under loose fabric. He ran my fingers along a hard, long bump. "How do you like that? We got a rib that's screwed up and touching my lung. Fell off of these steps," he gestured to the front door. "Got that rib pretty good, didn't it? They won't do nothing for that. You got to live with it."

He took a long drag and I watched the smoke curl in the unmoving air. On TV, Sean Hannity pursed his lips disapprovingly about the president. After a short silence Jim spoke again, quietly.

"I got so much I wanna do. Can't do it. A friend came over and said, 'You're not putting no garden in?' I said no. So he came back, tilled it, put it in for me. Now I go out there one day, like a stupid fool, and fell down in the middle of the garden and couldn't get up. I laid there for a half hour before they found me. I tried to crawl over to a fence. Couldn't even crawl. I wanted to plant . . . I think it was beans. All of a sudden my blood pressure was the problem."

I asked him if the place was really for sale. He nodded. He and Bertha, who'd had her own cancer scare in recent years, just weren't up for running it anymore. He was hoping to get $300,000, though no offers had come in yet. Potential buyers surely recognized that the initial overhead would be monumental: every aspect of the business could use upgrading and modernization, and that didn't even account for the unseen things that an inspection would reveal. Last year a man from my corner of Maryland's D.C. suburbs had come in with a friend and asked about buying it. Jim wasn't looking to sell at the time, and now that he was, he couldn't find the man's name or phone number among the mountains of decades-old paperwork that surrounded him in every room.

"He'll be back in the hunting season with his buddies, though," Jim told me with certainty.

Supposedly that mystery man wanted to keep the Troubadour as-is. Jim would hand him the keys and the music would keep going. But even if that were the case, it's no guarantee that the audience would be there to appreciate it.

"Last Saturday night, they told me they had sixteen ladies come in," Jim told me. "We gotta get that business. The locals don't have any money, they gotta drive to work, and D.C. or Hagerstown for big money. There ain't nothing here."

Another long silence settled in, and that was the most painful part of being in that trailer. Jim's life had revolved around sound — the pursuit of it, the creation of it, the capture of it, the business of it. A night owl, he was used to stepping outside in the darkness to hear the crickets buzzing in the mountain breeze. Now he woke at night and couldn't go anywhere, just lay in bed while the homeplace murmured beyond the trailer walls, awaiting a new owner who could tend to it properly.

"I'm just trying to get well," he told me. "And I will get well. I've made my mind up."

It's hard to watch an old person sit still when they plainly don't want to. Uncomfortable, I asked Jim if I could get him anything. He shrugged. Gave a sly fighter's smile.

"I like sitting back and talkin'."

8

※

Better Neighbors

A BRIGHT SATURDAY MORNING, BEFORE THE walking mall was even awake, before the shadows disappeared from Piccadilly Street, I parked and walked eagerly toward Just Like Grandma's, looking for my latest trip through Perry Davis's breakfast menu. His skills, as I'd learned on numerous mornings at the counter, extended past bacon and eggs, and I was dreaming of hot coffee and some time with a *Winchester Star* when I grabbed the door handle and found that it didn't budge. Through the glass, which I now realized had been scrubbed of the loopy scribbling that marked Perry's business, I could see three people, all young and white, spread throughout the room with brushes and paint rollers. One woman came over and unlatched the door.

"Is Perry here?" I asked, looking over the woman's shoulder

and noticing a blank white wall where the small stereo, newspaper clippings, and family photos once were.

"Who?" she asked. From the far side of the room, where I'd once seen a skeptical woman try her first hollandaise sauce, a man in jeans and a white T-shirt shouted, "He gave this place up."

"We open in two weeks," the woman said, smiling. "The Piccadilly Grill. Burgers and salads." I managed congratulations, and asked if she knew where to reach Perry.

"Try next door," she said. "The beauty school."

Ten feet away, another glass storefront window, this one filled with plants and a floor-length collection of sun-bleached close-ups of models with complicated '90s haircuts. I entered through a door underneath a humming air-conditioning unit and walked past a wall of shampoos and hair-spray cans to a large woman seated behind a desk.

"Perry?" she thought for a second when I asked about her former neighbor. "Think I heard he was cooking at the Twilight Zone now. You know where that is?"

I surely did. One of Joe Bageant's old hangs, on the southern end of downtown, right across the street from Gaunt's Drug Store, where Patsy used to serve ice cream. I thanked her and left, heading into the walking mall and past the coffee shop where I'd met Barbara Dickinson and watched the town's teens affect disaffection. Past the old Masonic hall and a brick building, now an antique store, with the midcentury painted logo for Sollenberger's Apples still preserved on the side. All the way to Cork Street, the mall's southern border, where a small stone building, purportedly George Washington's office during the French and Indian War, was open for business as a museum. Beyond Cork, the streets were leafy and residential, full of townhomes with small porches set back from the wavy, mossy brick sidewalks. Other than the cars lining both sides of the thin street, there was little to distinguish the scene from the 1950s. If you pined for a certain kind of past—one where neighbors borrow cups of sugar and chat on the sidewalk after they water their window boxes— you might feel that you'd found it here.

A couple blocks beyond that, where the trees became more sparse and the brick walks gave way to white concrete, I saw the Twilight Zone's small awning. Across the street, I saw that Gaunt's, still operational and owned by one of Patsy's old coworkers when I first started visiting a few years earlier, was now closed. Nothing had taken its place. The khaki-colored building sat tall in the midday sun, a FOR SALE sign leaned up against the front window where a Patsy cutout had once stood. On its side, the art deco–style metal lettering had been removed from the painted brick, leaving GAUNT'S DRUG STORE in a faint black outline.

The Twilight Zone had changed as well, from a certifiable dive bar into something more upscale called T-Bone's. Inside, a woman with chin-length hair was filling the glass racks and polishing the beer taps behind the bar. The Kardashians were arguing on a yacht on the TV when I sat down to ask about Perry.

"He doesn't really work here, but he uses our kitchen to cook for catering jobs sometimes. Want me to give him a call?" She scrolled through her phone and handed it to me when it started to ring. I told him he didn't know me but I was sorry to see his place go. Could he tell me why it happened?

"Tomorrow. I'll be there at noon," he said. "Come hungry."

When I showed up the next day a few minutes early, the manager had already brewed a pot of coffee. A few minutes past twelve, Perry opened the door and cast a broad stretch of day-light through the dim bar. He wore a tight blue T-shirt and ma-dras-patterned shorts and immediately asked if I'd eaten.

He disappeared into the kitchen and emerged ten long min-utes later with a bacon and egg sandwich that must have been half butter. I took a few bites and had to use multiple napkins to clean my hands. So, I asked him, how does cooking like this find itself homeless?

"My landlord," he explained. "It was one hassle after another. Those Historic District buildings are so outdated, and I wasn't getting no help from him. I had my refrigerators under the grill, where they have to work hardest to stay cool. The seals on them were old and particular. I had the AC go out, the water heater died, and I had to replace them myself. My lease included utili-ties but he wasn't paying any of them, and every time I signed a new one it was only for one year."

Despite his long, tight dreadlocks and slow, methodical speaking voice, he reminded me more than anyone of John, the old junk-store owner up on 522. Perry had gotten priced out of his business whereas John had simply been left to rot, but they shared the same businessman's despond, and a hypersensitivity to mistreatment. Perry had clearly itemized these issues before, to people who didn't have any reason to care. He told me more, about the effort he'd spent getting the diner's old vents and fix-tures professionally cleaned, the equipment he'd purchased out of pocket after his landlord refused to perform basic upkeep, the underhanded racism he experienced from his neighbors, who never so much as entered his restaurant to say hello or see his business up close. The bacon crunched in my mouth and I begged him to open another restaurant.

"I'm trying," he said. "Working with a realtor right now who's helping me find the right place. But I'm tired of Winchester. I'm tired of these closed minds, people just doing favors for their friends. I lost my spot because my landlord had friends who wanted it. Simple as that. There's a lot of old money here but very little worldliness or experience. My first cooking job was here, at the restaurant under the George Washington Hotel. My boss, he was trained, he knew how to cook. He came from Antigua and had a real proper European menu—béchamel sauces, swordfish paillard, real food. And then these rich people come in and mispronounced it all. They'd ask me what a 'beach-male' sauce was, then get mad when I explained it. They didn't want a black guy talking down to them."

He wanted to leave. Maybe to Savannah, Georgia, where he'd visited and seen plenty of the kind of restaurant he most wanted to own—soul food but done well, with proper care. What kept him in Winchester was the old woman who his short-lived business was named for: Viola Lampkin Brown, now 104 and still fiercely Christian. Perry explained that he'd grown up sitting on the floor of her house, watching her pray in a trance. These days she still did it, and she had plenty to pray for: Perry's mother was serving a thirty-year sentence for drug crimes in a federal prison in Connecticut, but the family had been mired in legal battles for years, arguing that her lawyer hadn't represented her properly. Finally in 2014, they received word that her sentence was one of hundreds being commuted by the Obama Justice Department, though she wouldn't be released for two more years, a few months after he and I were speaking. If she could make it to 106, Viola Lampkin Brown would get to see the granddaughter who she thought she'd lost for life. How could Perry leave her now?

"I just got my associate's degree in biblical studies," he went on. "To be honest I'm okay not cooking all the time. I'm trying to focus on congregation-building, kingdom-building. Any business I open will be a ministry. Gigi"—that's what he called his great-grandma—"instilled in me a sense of God's love and the power of living with that love. That's what I need to focus on now."

Perry's religious clarity notwithstanding, Just Like Grandma's had now joined the many other businesses I'd seen fall or shrivel in only my short few years traveling through greater Winchester. The Troubadour for sale, Gaunt's abandoned, John's Music on life support. The Royal Lunch, too, had served its last light beer. Even Covey Pro, the leading wrestling magnates of the eastern panhandle, had stopped putting on events by 2016. And Perry himself had become one of the struggling, searching iconoclasts that this place tended to breed, a black Joe Bageant with a spatula instead of a word processor, filling up the Twilight Zone with righteous anger. He had seen the ugly side of the place at close range and now couldn't see much else. All he wanted was a chance to serve other people and honor his family, but he was not the first person I'd met whose good intentions were strangled near George Washington's office and picturesque porches.

Perry was only the most recent of my acquaintances to talk about Winchester in terms of real estate and housing. After all, the town started as one man's property, and every sale since James Wood's initial offering to the government of Virginia slowly democratized it. The best way to assert oneself out here was to own a place, and no surprise, in a region with so much acreage and so much of the economy based on buying and selling and modernizing it, the local government and power structure were stocked with landlords and developers.

But by 2016 I'd gotten to know a young man with a much different perception of the relationship between "home" and mere ownership. Oscar Cerrito-Mendoza was first described to me as a quadruple minority—Latino, an immigrant, gay, and disabled. Perry may have stressed the town's closed-mindedness, but the word on Oscar was that he'd thrived in school and was now, in his early thirties, an accomplished professional and homeowner. In our initial conversations he had only smiles and gratitude for everyone he knew. On a late-March morning, I walked past Handley Library downtown and toward the squat building immediately to the west. This was Oscar's workplace, the dual headquarters for AIDS Response Effort and the Community Assistance Fund. ARE had been active since 1991 but just purchased this new property in 2015. The building used to be a bank, and the architecture had not changed. Even the drive-through teller window remained. By the front desk, floor-length windows filled the main lobby with light. The receptionist's chair was empty, and I heard nothing except a faint air-conditioner whirr, but the magazine racks and many open guest seats made it clear that this business saw plenty of traffic.

Oscar was in the basement, in one of a few windowless offices where his fellow do-gooders toiled. He sat upright, looking deeply into his computer, underneath an official certification from the Virginia Association of Housing Counselors. Beyond that, only a small stitched fabric pattern hung on the wall, beside a tall gray file cabinet. Oscar's ARE identification card hung around his neck on a lanyard against a blue button-down shirt. His right sleeve came down to his wrist, but the left was rolled up, an accommodation for his amelia—a congenital shortening of his arm about 4 inches past the elbow.

Oscar was at work on the unromantic nitty-gritty of social services: looking ahead, trying to make sure the grants overlapped, arranging for collaborations with bigger agencies. Nevertheless, he greeted me with the same disarming smile he always gave.

"We're still waiting for new rapid re-housing funding," he explained. "I'm trying to map out how the federal and state funds will cover things once the new grant cycle starts in July. Things are in a holding pattern now. Our intake and clinical side are hung up from the lack of funding."

Oscar had worked for ARE only a few years but he'd clearly developed a talent for the persistent, long-term vision that career social servants have to cultivate. He'd started by traveling in his car throughout the agency's purview, Lord Fairfax Health District number 7—including Clarke, Frederick, Page, Shenandoah, and Warren counties, as well as Winchester—finding people who needed housing. He'd since graduated to a coordinator, taking the wider view and supervising the efforts to get these homeless individuals into Winchester's meager supply of available beds. Having seen the structural difficulties inherent in that task, Oscar developed a centralized intake system: one protocol for every hospital, shelter, rehab clinic, and social agency to use for these men (they were almost always men) so that their case histories were more comprehensive.

He now had a larger dream: a shared database of individual case histories and available services, so any professionals in the continuum of care could see their clients' full journey and treatment so far. It was a data-driven approach that would be more useful if the supply of data were bigger. So Oscar's current project was to bring it to Valley Health, the enormous and growing corporation that owned Winchester Medical Center and many other facilities in the area. By this point, Valley Health was the greatest source of data and human services infrastructure in the region, with direct ties to every kind of facility from neonatal care to hospices. Not unlike the Latino population that came to the area purely for fruit picking, Valley Health had become an inextricable, built-in part of their community. And nobody embodied their simultaneous rise like Oscar.

He was born in San Juan del Llanito, Guanajuato, Mexico, in 1986, around the time that Jim and Bertha's neighbors were starting to visit the bar en masse. Oscar's father left for the United States shortly thereafter, and ended up working in a nursery in Texas. In San Juan, part of the flat arid desert about a hundred miles north of Mexico City, Oscar lived in poverty but with dignity and joy. Like Joe Bageant's, his was a life lived largely outdoors; the town was centered around a communal patio at the school which was filled on every holiday with big festivals of dancing, music, and food. Like a Berkeley Springs kid, he walked with his mother and two younger sisters to the nearby hot springs for water since it was cheaper than paying for tap. When money arrived from his father, they'd travel to the city for groceries, where mom would buy them chocolate-banana milkshakes as a treat.

On days when she worked as a maid, she left the kids with her own mother, but often grandma wouldn't stay the entire shift, so Oscar babysat for his sisters from the age of eight. He taught himself to cook the staples of those big communal parties: beans, fried eggs, tortillas. He warmed their unpasteurized milk on the stove to kill the bacteria.

Then in 1997, they were summoned. In late March, Oscar

joined his mother, two sisters, grandmother, and a male guide. They took a train from Querétaro to Nuevo Laredo, a border town where they slept overnight. In the morning they waded into the Rio Grande. The guide helped his grandmother, his mother helped the girls, and Oscar moved through the water while looking out for everyone. They stepped into Texas, and on the very first night, U.S. immigration police caught them and sent them back to Mexico. The following night, they made it across again, then the guide got lost on the U.S. side. The sun set as they wandered through the desert, then rose and set again as they wandered more. They had only enough food and water for two days, and they soon burned through that. They sneaked onto a farm and drank from a slimy cow's trough, the only water they could find. The guide stole food from a nearby house. Days later—impossible to say how many—another farmer took them in and gave them food and water to take. Then they pressed on, through pouring rain that soaked their clothes, blistering heat that dried everything through, then rain again. Oscar was stung by a wasp in a hunting cabin where they stopped for shade. He flicked away a scorpion before it had the same chance.

After days of desert toil and pilgrimage, they finally made it to a town near San Antonio and met Oscar's father, who said it had been a full week since he'd lost track of them. A full week with two barely school-age girls and an aged woman. He was already close to his mother but the experience bonded them for life. As an adult, he would still call her "my hero."

They had one night in San Antonio to bathe and rest in their first bed in a week. The next day it was off again, this time to West Virginia, where Oscar's paternal uncle was picking apples near Martinsburg. They drove up through coal country and into the Blue Ridge foothills and lived there in one room—three children and four adults, across three generations—while the men worked the harvest. In winter they moved to Hedgesville in the eastern panhandle, near Interstate 81.

Oscar spent a few weeks in the local elementary school, but no one spoke Spanish and he didn't know any English beyond "Hi, how are you?" He and his sister were transferred to Berkeley Springs Elementary because it had an ESL program, but even with the addition of the two Cerrito-Mendoza children, there were only four ESL students there.

It took Oscar one month to understand English and two to communicate with it himself. Just as he got on his feet, there was another move, this time to Clear Brook, in Frederick County, Virginia, north of Winchester. His uncle was now working on a dairy farm while his father picked apples and his mother sold homemade tamales and tacos at the orchards. Oscar drove all over with her to farms as far away as Stephens City whenever he was off school. The central migrant location was a former POW camp built during World War II, right by Byrd's processing facility, where the brick wall built by Jim McCoy's first guitar teacher still stood. The whole place—from the factory to the barbed-wire fence around the barracks—was now owned by White House, the national juice and sauce supplier. Oscar would go with his mother to this and other camps, interpreting when she spoke to orchard owners. By this point he was also interpreting at restaurants and doctors' offices for his parents, who had yet to become fully comfortable with the language. They had no time to learn: they were always working.

In his new school he was introduced to Katie Pitcock, the director of a migrant education program across the Winchester region. Pitcock was a white woman from Atlanta who arrived in Winchester in the mid-1970s just to drop a friend off there. Following the same wide-eyed, freewheeling sense of fate that brought Joe Bageant to Boulder and Jeanne Mozier to Berkeley Springs during the decade, Pitcock pulled into town at the height of the apple blossom bloom and simply knew this was where she needed to be. She applied for a job at the school district, which asked if she was willing to go into a migrant camp. None of their current employees were.

Pitcock soon became the migrant workers' advocate to the school board, rejecting, for example, the idea that they should simply have their own schools in their camps. She had pushed this rock uphill for more than a decade by the time she met Oscar, and could tell, even relative to the many resilient, inspiring children that she'd met over the years, that he was special. He had none of the usual shyness or meekness that she'd seen in so many Spanish-speaking kids. Instead, Oscar exuded an indefinable *presence*, an ability to disarm any situation. He laughed uproariously but focused when he needed to. She took him to an occupational therapist to help him better use his hand, and on the drive there he taught her a song in Spanish. He was barely eleven.

Despite Oscar's peripatetic couple of years, Pitcock credited his maturity to his rootedness. His family had fought to stay together. His parents were devoted and present. He had lived under the same roof as extended family, and once they arrived in the Virginias, they stayed. Many migrant families moved a seasonal circuit through the South, picking Florida oranges, Georgia peaches, and Shenandoah apples as the weather changed. Not so Oscar's family. They wanted steadiness and stability. They wanted to make a home.

They were not alone. By the twenty-first century, the Latino population in western Virginia was exploding. Between 1990 and 2000, the Hispanic share of Frederick County's census more than doubled; in Winchester city, it nearly sextupled. Oscar's family began attending Spanish-language services at Sacred Heart Church right across the street from Winchester Medical Center and down the road from the Museum of the Shenandoah Valley. It was a tiny congregation when they started, but a decade later it was standing-room only behind the back pews.

Over the course of that decade, Oscar grew into adulthood. In high school he grew to appreciate just how unique he was. More Hispanic kids kept arriving, but they usually came stateside at an older age than he was when he crossed the border. Especially after his accent subsided, he was caught in a no-man's-land: the white people all saw he was Mexican but the Latino kids considered him half-gringo. He began translating professionally, helping parents talk to teachers for Winchester public schools conferences. He also translated for clients at AIDS Response Effort, his first interaction with the group. And he finally came out as gay, drawing the Catholic ire of his beloved grandmother. She stopped speaking to him, and wouldn't again for years. But thanks to Katie Pitcock and the greater migrant education program, Oscar had dreams beyond family. He wanted to go to college. No one in his family had even graduated high school before. At home, too, he was both son and stranger.

He went to community college first and couldn't settle on a major, then went briefly to New York, thinking of a career in fashion. But before long he felt that southern pull, the undertow that tugs at country people when they roam. He also felt the gratitude of a survivor. Oscar had been helped by people who had made a life out of helping. He needed to give back, and he needed to do it in his own community.

"Our goal is a database of every open bed," he explained to me in his office. "There's always the problem of not enough beds."

I asked him who the Winchester homeless population tended to be. Was he drawn to that field because it was a chance to help fellow immigrants?

"Not at all," he said immediately. "In my time here, I've only seen one Hispanic homeless person, and he was undocumented, with no family. Mostly it's white people, either mothers with young kids fleeing abusive relationships, or white men with drug problems. Heroin is on the rise here. They've burned their bridges and have nowhere to go. In Winchester, homeless people are given shelter but little else. The government has its head in the sand. We need to provide them with wraparound services — shelter, but also employment counseling, medical care, mental health. Hispanic people can at least get help from their families. The Hispanic community is very supportive. People borrow money and stay close. Families understand the hardship."

I recalled the donation buckets at every outdoor Troubadour show — generously filled, but never enough to support Jim and Bertha as their bills mounted. I recalled the phrase with which Ernest Tubb, the man who invented postwar country, always ended his radio shows: "Be better to your neighbors and you'll have better neighbors, doggone you." But neighbors aren't the only thing that makes a neighborhood. Somebody has to own the buildings and pass the laws. And if they don't feel the need to treat anyone better, how much good can even the best neighbors do?

"I've had white clients that have so much shame," Oscar told me. "They've never had to ask for help before, and now they have to. The safety net is gone for them."

We left and went to a coffee shop across the street from the Handley Library, a gay-friendly place with a rainbow flag on the sign, called, ironically, The Hideaway. Within many residents' living memory, it was scandalous for women like Patsy Cline to be seen with married men on this very block.

The café was sleeker than the town's other latte haven around the corner, where I'd met Barbara Dickinson. The walls and tables were white, the décor more minimalist than purely cozy. It was empty other than a few college-age people with asymmetrical haircuts tapping away on laptops in beanbag chairs. Oscar ordered an herbal tea and we sat at a tall table.

He was thinking of an upcoming meeting with Valley Health. It would be only the latest of his many trips to the vast campus it occupied on the town's west side. For months now, he'd been traveling to the third floor of Medical Office Building 1, where a bright conference room with enormous windows looked out across Highway 37 onto rolling green hills that used to hold the world's most famous apple supply. There, along with Valley Health's clinical manager of social work and one or more representatives from the Winchester Free Medical Clinic, he would continue his efforts to improve and bridge the intake systems between the various members of Winchester's homeless continuum of care. They had already developed hospital protocols for the homeless population—whom to contact when a homeless person arrived in the emergency room, how to find an open bed, what questions to ask them about their past—and were now working on discharge standards. Oscar was also trying to figure out if Valley Health could, or would, help fund long-term housing solutions, whether by buying apartment buildings to use as shelters, or maybe setting up a field of tiny houses for the purpose. "Housing first," the notion that homeless people need a roof over their head before any other life improvements can take hold, had been gaining steam for years in social services. But housing is increasingly expensive, especially in a place like Winchester where the population is growing and real estate is a major path to wealth.

So why Valley Health? Ostensibly a medical organization, why would it play such a central role in finding beds for the homeless? The obvious reason is money. Every homeless-serving agency on earth has to fund-raise, and Valley Health, which operates six hospitals and innumerable family and specialist offices throughout the region, reported more than $782 million in revenue in 2015; any local agency with any sense would approach its charitable foundations with hat in hand.

But there were other reasons for Valley Health to worry about housing. A homeless person is more likely to get sick, and less likely to have insurance coverage, meaning they are an expensive potential customer—no insurer will be picking up the tab, and Valley Health has to pay for their care out of a special fund for unavoidable or charitable costs. The homeless are also more likely to return to the hospital chronically, which makes them doubly expensive. For years, the quality of a hospital's care was gauged according to straightforwardly calculable things like the average length of patients' stays. But the Affordable Care Act changed the determinant of medical quality to ineffable things like "population health," including readmissions, the frequency with which patients return for additional care within thirty days of being treated. Beginning October 1, 2012, right as Oscar started working with the homeless, the Centers for Medicare and Medicaid Services began lowering payment rates for hospitals with excess readmissions. Too many people coming back too quickly, and CMS would reimburse for all patients at a lower rate. And in 2016, Valley Health recorded 56 homeless hospital patients who totaled 193 visits — an average of 3 or 4 visits a year per individual, and that's not including those who use the emergency room.

A cynical person might therefore note that helping the homeless helps Valley Health's bottom line. But it's also a worthwhile investment for a company designed for nonstop growth. From colonial settlers to General Sheridan, the Shenandoah has been prone to occasional takeover, but since its founding in 1994, Valley Health has managed one of the grandest in history. The company was inaugurated through the merger of a health services business and a transportation company, which incorporated and purchased Winchester Medical Center, built in 1903, where Patsy Cline and countless other locals were born. It quickly purchased other smaller hospitals around the region, such as the fourteen-bed facility Hampshire Memorial, out near Bertha's hometown of Romney, West Virginia. Valley Health then started buying out independent family medicine offices, then specialist practices. It opened fitness centers and hosted wellness events. Being exempt from real state or corporate income taxes, it made hundreds of millions from these holdings, and being nonprofit, it had to funnel the money back into business. And so it expanded steadily and constantly, adding multimillion-dollar cancer and heart centers to its main campus, opening a members-only gym, and establishing strategic partnerships with local schools and colleges to improve science classes and career preparations. It is an annual corporate benefactor of the Apple Blossom Festival, where it sponsors a 10K race. Valley Health, in other words, has turned itself into an omnipresent force in Winchester residents' lives, an unavoidable partner from cradle to grave. Not even Harry Flood Byrd managed such a widespread presence, though surely he'd be pleased to know that his grandson, Harry F. Byrd III, has served on the boards of directors for Valley Health and Winchester Medical Center.

Despite all this, its nonprofit status means Valley Health is still exempt from taxes on its growing real estate footprint and its corporate income. This has led to ongoing arguments about the actual monetary advantage it provides to Winchester. It claimed a total of $118 million in "community benefit dollars" in 2015, a mixture of charity care, educational offerings, and Medicare shortfall. And it must be noted that greater Winchester, unlike many rural areas in the United States, still has hospitals. More than eighty rural hospitals have closed since 2010, and among those that remain, 41 percent have a negative profit margin. So far, Valley Health has kept the worst of rural American health crises at bay.

But heroin and opioids, according to Oscar and others, are on the rise, and are major drivers of homelessness. Obesity, hypertension, high cholesterol, and dental problems are the lot of America's lower classes, and Winchester's are not exempt. And despite Valley Health's growing physical and economic presence in the community, plenty of its active and potential patients struggle to pay their bills, even with insurance. With their ongoing procession of lung, bone, heart, and circulatory problems, Jim and Bertha became chronic readmissions to Winchester Medical Center once they exhausted Dr. Matt Hahn's ability to treat them in his family practice in Hancock, Maryland. The McCoys were Medicaid recipients who had accounted for a portion of the wealthy hospital's tally of "community benefit dollars" for years, yet they still fund-raised from their friends and concertgoers to avoid bankruptcy.

As the new ACA laws took hold and Valley Health's domination of the upper Valley proceeded apace, Dr. Hahn watched Jim, Bertha, and their fellow high-need rural patients leave his independent practice for the plusher confines of Winchester Medical Center and other Valley Health facilities, often by going into deep debt. His own independent practice, too, was newly overwhelmed by the increasing levels of paperwork and technology fees required by the regulations; the push for multifaceted "population health" meant more bookkeeping and more mandated activities, like setting up online health portals and communicating with a minimum number of patients by e-mail. This in addition to the recurring nightmare of dealing with insurance and medical billing companies to discern every patient's level of coverage and pricing. Hahn's frustrations became the impetus for a book, *Distracted: How Regulations Are Destroying the Practice of Medicine and Preventing True Health-Care Reform,* which he published in 2017.

Despite its subtitle, Hahn's book is not a conservative jeremiad in favor of general deregulation. Instead, it is a cry against the corporatization of medicine and the federal government's seeming support for it. After all, their booming, tax-exempt revenues allow conglomerates like Valley Health to absorb all the new paperwork and managerial tasks with relatively little effort—hiring additional workers to make calls and fill out forms all day even counts toward their community benefit. Hahn doesn't mention Valley Health by name, but his book is a point-by-point tour of the medical industry to convey "the need for government regulation, *good* government regulation, to protect citizens from the consequences of uncontrolled corporate greed." In *Deer Hunting with Jesus,* Joe Bageant essentially described Valley Health as a federally funded Walmart of medicine, with an economic mandate to absorb everything in sight. Ten years later, even after new Democrat-sponsored legislation to improve health-care insurance coverage among low-income people, Hahn's own book showed how the situation had only grown worse.

Oscar had as much knowledge of these complications as anyone can, yet he maintained his social worker's optimism. "I like it here," he told me. "I like the festivals, they remind me of home." He had recently returned from his youngest sister's quinceañera, back in Mexico. "And it's nice that Winchester remains pretty locally owned."

He wasn't wrong. The business that had taken Perry's place wasn't a chain. Few of the shops or restaurants on the walking mall were corporate, either. But the same chamber of commerce that recognized the appeal of a quaint, homey shopping district also recognized the value of an enormous mall just outside town, and acres upon acres of big-box shopping surrounding it. In either case, the regional economy, like the national one, was forever tipping toward corporate benefit.

This was the world that Oscar had inherited in Winchester: more diverse and accepting in many ways, but still stratified, and the people on the lower strata were still clinging by their fingernails. It wasn't impossible to start an independent business—for most minorities especially, it was easier than ever, just as there were now more resources for non-English-speaking children. But every component of the economy, from the rising value of land to the cost of well-intentioned regulations, makes owning that business more difficult than it used to be.

I asked Oscar if he suffered from burnout, a common affliction for social workers. Do the drug casualties and the lost lives weigh on him day after day?

"It can be hard," he admitted, "though I'm committed to this. When I get home, I like to cook. That's what brings me joy. Making the food that I had growing up. And when the job becomes frustrating, I do have a fantasy of doing that full-time. My dream job," he said with his usual bashful grin, "is to open a restaurant."

Late summer 2016. Friends had installed a plywood ramp leading up to Jim and Bertha's front door, and a midafternoon storm had made it slick and smooth. Up I went, knocking before entering immediately; I'd been told that Jim wouldn't be able to get up and let me in.

He was in a wheelchair in the kitchen, near the card table covered in documents and printouts and envelopes from Valley Health. He looked collapsed inside a white T-shirt and pajama pants, but his eyes brightened when he saw me. The barest curl of a smile, bordered, as I'd never seen before, by white stubble. He took my hand and gripped it gently in his bloodless fingers. I held on as I sat down in a lawn chair by the table and looked into his worried eyes. Sean Hannity was shaking his head on a TV above the couch.

"Got Penny here," he said, referring to his daughter who was visiting from San Diego. She'd been there since March, when a fresh round of hospitalizations began. Jim was at the point in his sickness when he needed surgeries to recover from surgeries. Treatment for a fall left him bruised and swelling. Swelling made it harder to move and breathe. The lack of movement weakened and demoralized him.

Other losses did as well. On November 7, he'd spoken with Charlie Dick, just as they did a few times a week.

"He was telling me about NASCAR," Jim said. "Talking to me about the new cars. Then the next day I got that call." Charlie died in his sleep, eighty-one years old. The burial was back at Shenandoah Memorial, and Jim and Bertha made it down. Julie invited them to sit with family for the service.

Buddy Emmons, Ernest Tubb's pioneering pedal steel player, had died a few months before Charlie, and Merle Haggard died a few months after. Fittingly, Jim had the past in mind. He wanted to tell me about booking Waylon Jennings for a concert near Winchester in the early 1970s. He wanted me to know about the old-time banjo player Wade Mainer, about the religious singer Jimmy Miller, about the greatness of cowboy balladeer Marty Robbins. I asked when he was happiest.

"When we first came up here," he said. "Only had one thing to take care of."

Was he scared?

"Nope. I've had a good life. You gotta get ready. I hope people remember me for being a good man. For being a family man."

Penny arrived, walking through the door with a woman I recognized from the restaurant. Behind them came the other woman's husband, in a camouflage coat. They all smelled of cigarettes, which made Jim reach for his. He couldn't light it, just held it in his mouth and sat the lighter in his lap.

"They brought you something, Dad," Penny told him, sitting on the couch and turning down the television.

"You said you needed a new belt for that mower," said the camouflaged man, offering Jim a plastic bag from a local hardware store. Jim seemed awestruck. He reached for his wallet.

"C'mon now," the woman said. "Let us do something for you." Bertha entered now too, perpetually shaking her head about the business. Her dog, a little yappy white thing, ran up to her eagerly.

"Y'all got him that?" she asked the visitors. They nodded. "Too good to us," she said. She went over to the couch and put a loving arm around Penny, whose long wavy brown hair fell over her shoulders.

"I don't know what we'd be doing without Penny these months," she told me. Penny took her hand and they leaned their heads together.

The gift-bearing friends wished everyone a good night and Penny yawned, arms outstretched. Bertha retired to a reclining chair and yanked the handle hard to pop the leg support out. The dog jumped on her and positioned his belly for scratching. She obliged. Jim turned up the TV as a panel argued over footage of Hillary Clinton waving from a tarmac.

"Who you votin' for, John?" Bertha asked. The election was in less than three months. I admitted the truth: a fully brainwashed East Coast liberal, I supported the lady on the tarmac, mainly out of fear of the competition. Bertha laughed and shook her head.

"I don't know about them," she said, trailing off.

"Hillary," Jim said skeptically. Then, after a minute, "I don't trust her." Their skepticism didn't surprise me. This was a common refrain that summer, and not only among poor white people in trailers, though the focus and the blame seemed to always be on them. What had any Clinton done to improve life on Highland Ridge, anyway? What story or vision of this country could a career politician tell to Jim McCoy? A lifetime of obstinate individualism and geographic dislocation had left Jim beyond the reach of traditional political platitudes. No one in that realm spoke his language, but at least Fox was easy to understand.

I didn't want to go. I didn't know if I could handle saying good-bye to Jim this time. I stopped talking, and let this exhausted family simply sit and rest, unconcerned with hospitality for once. On the lounger, rubbing softly behind her grateful dog's ears, Bertha watched the news, rapt.

9

Blessed to Be Gray

On Wednesday, September 7, 2016, about 300 years to the day since the Knights of the Golden Horseshoe crossed the Swift Run Gap, an enormous storm rolled over the northern Shenandoah and approached the Blue Ridge Mountains, headed east. Massive churning clouds, dark black and blue, billowed and flashed with veins of jagged lightning. The kind of nightmare storm that every mountain resident has in the back of their mind when they scan the sky: Wagnerian rain, root-ripping wind, and close, quaking thunder.

Penny watched it approach. She was outside having a cigarette and taking a break from Jim's bedside. The weekend before had been Labor Day, the first without Charlie, though the Sunday party went on as usual. Jim had made a brief appearance, almost an apparition, guided by Bertha and the hospice nurse that had moved in with them a few days earlier. Penny was scheduled to return to California by the end of the week, but everything had slowed down. They were going hour to hour now, seeing if Jim made one of his trademark recoveries. Just a minute before she'd stepped outside, Jim was on the phone with one of the bands he booked regularly at the Troubadour.

The rain picked up, and Penny returned to the house. When she came in, she saw Bertha's face, and she knew.

The word got out through the Troubadour Facebook page in early evening, then out through the Celebrating Patsy Cline page and Twitter account, and through a series of phone calls stretching from Highland Ridge to San Diego, Nashville, Winchester, and all points beyond where people felt invested in the saga of Patsy Cline. I was under an awning in the D.C. suburbs, my hair flattened by rain after a miscalculated attempt to cross a parking lot at the tail end of the storm. Soaked through, my shoes now squishing with every step, I took refuge in a dry spot and pulled my phone out to check for damage. I scrolled through messages and saw one spare note from the Patsy folks: beloved friend, Joltin' Jim McCoy, has passed away at home. Arrangements to come. Attached was a picture I hadn't seen, a 1960s black and white press photo from J&J Talent Service in Winchester, showing Jim seated with a big blond acoustic guitar balanced between his knees and his name emblazoned on the strap. Rhinestone musical notes wound up his sleeves and across his suit jacket and a pristine white cowboy hat was perched atop his head, curled up at the edges like a soaring manta ray. His face was confident but unsmiling, and his left hand, resting on his left knee, looked veiny, dark, and muscular. He looked as sharp and stunning as a navy cadet. The last burbles of thunder rolled away and I looked at this picture, marveling that even though I'd only known him as a frail old man, this was still the vision of him that I carried in my head. Even slow, sick, and dying, he always sat at the center of a world he'd made.

It took nearly a week for the funeral arrangements to come together. Finally, on September 13, an overflow crowd gathered at the Carlyle Chapel in the Helsley-Johnson Funeral Home on the northern end of Berkeley Springs. It was a Tuesday morning during the early school year, so the neighborhood was mostly empty. I parked near the 7-Eleven and waited for a hauling truck to cut through Washington Street so I could cross. The line of mourners stretched onto the funeral home's wooden porch stairs. Inside, there were dozens of family members, all the way down to great-great-grandchildren, along with plenty of friends and locals. Jim lay in repose, in a suit and boutonniere, casket open. The lights were low and the textured ceiling was speckled with small shadows. Bertha was up front in black, near the twins.

I took a seat in one of the folding chairs the funeral home had added to the chapel lobby. I didn't see many suits or dresses around me. Two young men sat next to each other with Metallica T-shirts visible under their untucked Western wear. I was next to a table with a guest book and a picture of Jim wearing the cowboy hat and guitar-patterned collared shirt that he'd worn the first weekend I met him. In the photo he looked strong and barrel-chested, though it couldn't have been taken more than a couple years before I arrived.

Bertha's son, Pastor Andy Shanholtz, presided over the service. He'd come in from Sheboygan, Wisconsin, where he'd made his home for decades — far from the tumult of his childhood, by design. But he spoke of Jim lovingly.

"Ever the showman, Jim sat down with me in 2012 with the plans he'd made for this service," he said. "Every song today, every reading, is Jim's choice."

And in full Joltin' Jim style, he played the hits, starting with Psalm 23, read by the pastor. Then came Patsy's version of "Just a Closer Walk with Thee," her subdued but bouncing march recorded with the Jordanaires. It played over the small black speakers mounted in the corners of the room, and was immediately followed by "She's the Best," which Jim had written later in his life for Bertha. The recording was Jim's own, his wobbly, elderly baritone playing above the crack Troubadour Studios band. It was a slow waltz, devotional, walking through a day of domestic tranquility from morning coffee onward. The chorus was the classic country kind: a sudden harmonic leap up and slow descent down, guided by Jim's repeated praise: "She's the best I'll ever do." Then finally, Jim and Charlie's duet on "Waltz Across Texas." It was a recent recording, and neither of them were able to project and sustain very well. But it was all the more poignant to hear these two men, now both ghosts, creak and groan like this. They'd outlasted bigger legends and brighter talents, and seen many of the greatest up close. But they also knew that music was, at root, just a way for people to be together. It was an excuse to communicate, to share, to celebrate.

After a reading of James 4:14 — "You do not even know what will happen tomorrow. What is your life? You are a mist that appears for a little while and then vanishes"—Pastor Shanholtz commenced his recollections. His memories were all of light and growth: Jim loved family time, especially Christmas, and had to hang those strands of rainbow bulbs everywhere he could fit them. "He could grow plants in clay," as well; gardening was second only to his passion for music. In work and in life, Jim wanted roots, wanted color, wanted the maximum possible atmosphere of comfort and sustenance. In the pastor's words, "Jim never lost a friend."

We all stood and marched single file to see the coffin up close and pay our respects to Bertha and the family. Our soundtrack for this walk was "I Fall to Pieces," Patsy's second, career-making hit. I was surprised by the choice. Jim had told me more than once that his favorite Patsy song was "Three Cigarettes in an Ashtray," an archetypal lost-love weeper. And of course, "San Antonio Rose" was the one he heard her sing first. But instead he chose this song, a loping oldies radio staple from 1961. Unlike "Crazy," released the following year, "I Fall to Pieces" was only three chords, a perfectly straightforward honky-tonk song. No complex phrasings or melodic leaps, just a steady and persistent rhythm track over a graceful vocal line that rose and fell one word at a time. But the meaning of any song will change when you hear it near an open casket, and approaching my departed friend I heard fresh nuances in the song's lyrics. The central metaphor of collapse, of course, sounded now like a comment on old age or the rural culture that the Troubadour embodied. But falling to pieces is only a response to the song's central concern —the narrator is really plagued by memory: "You want me to act like we've never kissed . . . But you walk by and I fall to pieces." It is a song about the past, about feelings so intense that they can weaken a person in an instant, out of nowhere. It is a song about the tragic flip side to having deep roots: they can keep you from moving on.

I took my last steps up to the casket and saw Jim's emotionless, vaguely plastic face. He looked healthy again, but not himself. He was not meant for lying down. He should be out, living among his memories and helping others create their own. His heroism, and the heroism of all classic country songs, was his persistence. Life can be painful, but it must be embraced. Love can kill us, but there's nothing better. There are so many forces pushing us into the future whether we like it or not, burying orchards and homesteads under highways and megastores. But the homesteads were still there, they were worth fighting for and singing about. Everything falls to pieces, but don't act like you've never kissed.

We had a police escort down to the Virginia line, at which point the dark green Econoline van containing Jim's casket took the lead to Shenandoah Memorial Park. It took ten minutes for the line of cars to make it into the parking lot. Then we gathered around the site by the entrance road, just a few yards over from Patsy and Charlie. I recognized people I hadn't seen in years: the huge man who sang about Jesus at my first karaoke night; Sandy Uttley, whose Patsy tribute CD Jim had recorded and won awards for; Tracie Dillon, a former Celebrating Patsy Cline board member who had spoken in the chapel at this very location for the fiftieth memorial; and Julie Fudge, Patsy's daughter, back in Winchester for a funeral once again.

There were few tears. These last months had been hard, and uncertainty loomed about Bertha and the homeplace. The rumor was that she intended to keep the business going at least through the following summer, though everyone knew that a lot could change. The gathering around Jim's grave site was full of hugs and recollections, and old people pulling grandchildren close to explain the old days.

Eventually, Pastor Shanholtz called everyone in and pulled a white piece of paper from his leather notebook. It was a typed message from Jim, which he'd asked to have delivered at his burial. Over the quiet rustling leaves and the sound of nearby cars, we heard Joltin' Jim's final testimony:

> I am so blessed to have lived long enough to have my hair turning gray, and to have my youthful laughs forever etched into deep grooves on my face. So many have never laughed, and so many have died before their hair could turn silver. As you get older, it is easier to be positive. You care less about what other people think. I don't question myself any more. I've even earned the right to be wrong.
>
> So, to answer your question, I like being old. It has set me free. I like the person I have become. I'm not going to live forever, but while I am still here, I will not waste my time lamenting what could have been, or worrying about what will be. And I shall eat dessert every single day (if I feel like it). MAY OUR FRIENDSHIP NEVER COME APART, ESPECIALLY WHEN IT'S STRAIGHT FROM THE HEART.

Jim had bought this plot years ago, after burying Patsy and his son Andrew in the same ground. He'd since buried Charlie, along with many other friends and family, adding up to more than five decades, two-thirds of his life, spent in recurring grief and remembrance on this one loping field. It sounds tragic, but cemeteries aren't only for mourning; they are defenses against time, claiming a landscape against further change. This particular cemetery was acres wide, bordered by single-family homes on all sides, including a neighborhood of prefabricated mansions just west. But in fifty years, no section of Winchester will look more well preserved or timeless than Shenandoah Memorial Park. As we listened to Jim's last words, the ultimate fate of the

Troubadour remained unclear. But Jim would rest here, south of Winchester, among his most dearly missed friends, for as long as this land existed. Mourning allows for constancy, something that this region — this country — often precludes.

Despoliation, the plunder of once-pure things, is the most American song of all. No city is ever as good as it once was, and every old man can regale you with tales of days gone by. Imagine what unblemished beauty Alexander Spotswood beheld as he crested the Swift Run Gap, or what it must have been like to hear Patsy Cline's voice soaring in some nondescript roadhouse before the world knew her name. We take it for granted that our mania for new buildings and new fortunes deprives us of these experiences, then we romanticize the rediscovery of what we've lost. A house that looks just like a country legend's. A luxury spa scene to rival Berkeley Springs's early days. A farmers' market to sell the kind of heirloom produce that every family used to grow as a matter of course.

We know, too, that all this change and loss leave tragedies in their wake. Factories close or an industry dies, neighborhood businesses lose out to chains, and the people around them are left desperate and isolated. And so we convince ourselves they deserved it: they're uneducated, or uncouth, or addicted to the wrong kinds of drugs. We pathologize. We look for justifications and treat each left-behind community like a self-contained case. In many ways, Jim was a left-behind person. The music industry he loved outgrew his style and never returned his devotion. His rural community collapsed, a victim of modernization. Then his health faltered and his businesses struggled, as happened to so many country people around him. He had a drawl, and a home that might have been featured in a glossy magazine article about the rural poor. Yet over the course of my time around him,

Jim's life only came to seem more and more similar to mine. He fought against mounting bills and tried to keep his family intact. For a time, a long time, he managed that. He sold records and songs and sandwich meat and beer, and finally opened a place that granted people a rare view of the way things used to be. He showed me that the left-behind people aren't mere victims. They are trying to make a life in a world where the good old days are gone. What could be more purely American?

There was talk around the grave site of the reception back up at the Troubadour. There would be a potluck and eventually, inevitably, music. Today would be purely celebratory, a respite from the ongoing sense of impending loss that had settled there. There would be time for that later, because in our country, it's always the end of something.

I dropped my bag on the bed and looked out the window onto Washington Street. A mid-December ice storm the previous night had turned the road to a slick, wet mess. My room, one of five cozy low-lit hideaways on the second floor of a Berkeley Springs restaurant, looked like a spot where you might take refuge with a briefcase full of money and a dangerous woman. Briefly, I washed my face and looked at the bathroom's floral print wallpaper, the musty pillows on the tall bed. Then down to the restaurant bar for a coffee to stay awake.

"The Troubadour?" asked the young woman in a waist-apron and embroidered polo shirt as I took my first sip. It was as if I'd told her I was in town to swim the frozen Potomac. "What's going on up there?"

"There's a band tonight actually."

"Really? I didn't even know they had music anymore. I've never been there."

Her loss. The band was from Baltimore, a country-rock trio that kept bottles of beer on the amps, wobbling precariously as their racket shook the stage. The singer spoke of what a privilege it was. Dr. Matt Hahn was there with friends, dancing and shouting on the checkerboard main floor. Codi couldn't pour the Rocket Fuel fast enough. I hadn't seen it this raucous in ages. It was as if Jim's death had released the place from its obligation to seriousness. We were no longer waiting around for the end of an era. A new one could commence, come what way.

Bertha stopped in for a second, greeting me with a big hug of the sort I'd seen her lavish on beloved guests on my first night. She was surviving, she said. Taking one day at a time. I couldn't help but tell her: I missed him. She took my hand and guided me over to a picture of Jim near the door. "He's still here," she said, hugging my shoulders. "I know that for sure."

A good crowd, bigger as the night wore on. A whole separate party raged around the pool tables, deep-toned screams of delight with every victory and especially every embarrassment. Dozens of empty glasses covered every table, surrounding half-finished pitchers like worshippers around an idol. All the pool players wore baseball hats, most of them camouflaged. Between songs a fight broke out between two girls in equally ill-fitting tops. It was about a boy, a smooth-faced young man who looked barely old enough to drive. Tammy, Codi's normally all-smiles partner at the bar, had to break it up with a few hard slaps on the counter and threats to kick them all out. An hour later, one girl hit her Rocket Fuel limit and ended up weeping on another man's shoulder. When she left, escorted through the crowd by a protective friend, her face was one puffy smear of tears and mascara.

All the way till midnight, three-plus hours of sweaty work by the band. They closed with a riotous final chord, held forever, the drummer tumbling and whipping at his kit before lifting the sticks and bringing everything to a close with one final triumphant blast. Then the clapping, the stomping, begging, before Codi called it all to order and made us close out. It was almost Christmas. Everyone tipped heavy and threw another couple bucks in the big plastic jar for Bertha's medical bills, or a new roof, or whatever they might need it for up here.

Outside, "on the wide level of a mountain's head," as Coleridge put it, the good-byes were sloppy and quick in the freezing parking lot. The Troubadour's huge neon sign was brighter than the full moon but only barely. Then the familiar left turn onto Highland Ridge Road, putting the moon on my right. I rolled the window down a little and got that frigid mountain air on my face. Past the new neighbors and a construction site I'd never seen before this visit—they were fixing the one-lane bridge and had cleared out a corner of the woods to make room for bulldozers and piles of steel beams. Down past the artificial ponds, partly frosted-over, the garages and porches, following the path that water would take if a spring suddenly sprang from the McCoy property. A raccoon stole across the road, turning its head just enough to catch my lights in its glowing mirrored eyes. Soon enough it was gas stations and streetlamps and resorts once again. Back on earth. Until next time.

Acknowledgments

If I'm being honest, this entire project began as an excuse to hang out with Matt Yake, who joined me on my initial trips to Winchester and the Troubadour and on many more over the next four years. His photographs and conversation have helped me see this place and these people in ways that I wouldn't have otherwise. It's an honor to have his work and his name in these pages.

No one has ever worked harder on my behalf than David Patterson. That makes him a great agent, but his kindness and support during the writing of this book have made him a trusted friend. Ben Hyman, meanwhile, saw the import and drama in Jim McCoy's story and convinced me it was worth telling at such length. This would be a lesser book—and I would be a lesser writer—without him. I owe these two gentlemen the world.

I am so grateful to have found a home for this book at Houghton Mifflin Harcourt, where Nicole Angeloro guided me to the finish line with care and insight. Thank you to her and to Bruce Nichols, Martha Kennedy, Beth Burleigh Fuller, Chrissy Kurpeski, and Elizabeth Pierson for the incredible thoughtfulness and attention that I was given from the get-go. What an absolute thrill to work with people who respect readers and authors so much.

Thanks to Marisa Carroll and Steve Kandell at BuzzFeed; John Summers, Thomas Frank, and Lindsey Gilbert at *The Baffler*; and especially Andrew Womack and Kate Ortega at *The Morning News*, who edited and published essays that grew into chapters herein.

Many people welcomed me into their homes and/or talked at generous length about their complicated hometown. A few I feel indebted to for life: Wil Cather, Nick Smart, Katie Pitcock, Kent Mull, Jodi Young, JudySue Huyett-Kempf, Phil Glaize III, Andy Gyurisin, Warren Hofstra, John Douglas, Dr. Matt Hahn, and Russell Mokhiber. Among the many people I've written about in these pages, I am particularly grateful to Barbara Dickinson and Oscar Cerrito-Mendoza, who were unbelievably patient and generous as I poked and prodded their personal lives for years. I only hope I have repaid your trust and openness.

Supreme thanks to a few guys whose excitement and support have meant everything: Ted Scheinman, Elon Green, Dave Stack, Burke Sampson, Pat Jarrett, Daniel Polansky, Pete Backof, Will Crain, and Alex Cameron. May your music always be loud and your beer always be cold.

Thanks are not enough for my mom and dad, who taught me to love reading and music, and have been incredibly supportive in all my efforts with both over the years. In so many ways, this book is a tribute to them. Ditto for Ishai, Anna, and Jake, wonderful siblings who have always taken such joy from my enthusiasms and given me so much to be proud of in return. To Denise, and to my extended families in the United States and Poland: you have enriched my life beyond measure and your support means everything. I love all of you.

To my beloved young readers, Nina and Albert: this is where Daddy was all those nights. I hope this book exhibits a little of your curiosity and kindness. I am amazed by you every day.

And of course to Justyna, who carried this book on her back as long as I did. Who watched our kids on her own as I drove around in search of a mercurial story hours away. Who endured my growing obsession with "twangy" music. Who deserves much more than just a dedication in a book. As Patsy wrote to her mama: We made it. *Kocham cię.*

Notes on Sources

Preface

My main source on the Knights of the Golden Horseshoe and the early development of Winchester is *The Planting of New Virginia* (2004) by Warren R. Hofstra, a leading historian of the region who teaches at Shenandoah University and once kindly met me for coffee. For the changing face of Winchester, I relied on U.S. Census Bureau figures and a Winchester-Frederick County Chamber of Commerce document called "Facts from Figures" (2006), as well as the area's Manufacturing Directory (2012).

That breathless Wordsworth line is taken from the first poem in his collection *Poems on the Naming of Places* (1800).

Chapter 1: The Blue Ridge Country King

For the origins of honky-tonk country, the place to start is Bill C. Malone's epochal *Country Music, U.S.A.* (1968; multiple editions ever since), the first major scholarly historical treatment of the genre. Malone has written many additional books, of which *Don't Get above Your Raisin': Country Music and the Southern Working Class* (2002) proved most illuminating for this project. Additional insights and biographical information about Ernest Tubb are available in Peter Guralnick's *Lost Highway* (1979); Guralnick's two-volume biography of Elvis Presley (*Last Train to Memphis* [1994] and *Careless Love* [1999]) contains vivid descriptions of the early rock 'n' roll record and touring industries as well. For sheer fun, any reader interested in the formation and character of those industries should read Nick Tosches's *Country* (1977) and *Unsung Heroes of Rock 'n' Roll* (1984). It was Tosches who identified the late-Victorian appearance of the phrase "honky-tonk." Another invaluable font of information here is John Broven's magisterial *Record Makers and Breakers* (2008), particularly the "Hillbilly Boogie" chapter.

For this and subsequent chapters relating Jim McCoy's biography, I am supremely indebted to John Douglas's *Joltin' Jim: Jim McCoy's Life in Country Music (2007)*, a spirited and well-researched biography that you can find in greater Winchester's finer gift shops and bookstores. There is also a biographically informative video interview with Jim on the website Morgan County, USA. For scenic descriptions of life on Highland Ridge in the immediately pre- and postwar eras, I relied heavily on *Rainbow Pie: A Redneck Memoir* (2010), the memoir of

Jim's neighbor, Joe Bageant. There is more on Joe's books in the notes for Chapter 6.

Information on the early days of WINC was gathered from "WINC-FM—The First 50 Years, 1946-1996," in the Stewart Bell Archives of the Handley Regional Library.

Chapter 2: A Closer Walk with Thee

The first biography of Patsy Cline was Ellis Nassour's *Honky-Tonk Angel* (1981), though I found more use for Margaret Jones's *Patsy: A Life of Patsy Cline* (1994), which seems to be the preference for most devotees I've met. (Conjecture and grapevine tales are preferable to books for most of these folks, however.) As I say, Douglas Gomery's *Patsy Cline: The Making of an Icon* (2011) is exceptional for his insights into Patsy's very early life and love of jazz, as well as his depiction of her posthumous career as a cultural totem and signifier. Naturally, Loretta Lynn's *Coal Miner's Daughter* (1976) contains some beloved descriptions of Patsy the friend and vulnerable star, and you can find additional early-'60s Nashville memories in Willie Nelson's *It's a Long Story* (2015) and Johnny Cash's *Cash: The Autobiography* (1997).

There is a preponderance of additional published material on Patsy's life, including *Love Always, Patsy: Patsy Cline's Letters to a Friend* (1999), if you want a taste of her epistolary talents; *Patsy Cline: Singing Girl from the Shenandoah Valley* (1996), which features some nice photos and region-specific stories; and *The Airplane Crash That Killed Patsy Cline* (2011), an e-book that features exacting mechanical triage of the crash itself, if that's what you're after. Serious fans should also track down *The Patsy Cline*

Collection box set (1991), featuring all 102 sides she recorded in her career, as well as expert liner notes by Paul Kingsbury.

Sweet Dreams: The World of Patsy Cline (2013), edited by Warren R. Hofstra, features essays that have enhanced this book from all angles, particularly its wealth of information about Winchester's midcentury social customs.

The details of George Washington's cursed stay (and exploitative redemption) in pre-Revolutionary Winchester are drawn from Ron Chernow's *Washington: A Life* (2010), though you can find them repeated and embellished in most local guidebooks and historical pamphlets.

Chapter 3: Resistance

My main source for the early history of Virginia's apple cultivation is an article by S. W. Fletcher, "A History of Fruit Growing in Virginia," from *Proceedings of the 37th Annual Meeting of the Virginia Horticultural Society, 1932*. For the Valley's apple industry, specifically its recent decline, I relied on Scott Hamilton Suter's introduction to Scott Jost's handsome photo book *Shenandoah Valley Apples (2013)*. Henry Adams's note about Virginians is from *The Education of Henry Adams* (1902).

Unsurprisingly, I also found plenty of fruit material in the books that detailed Harry Flood Byrd's greater life and career: Ronald L. Heinemann's *Harry Byrd of Virginia* (1996) and *Depression and New Deal in Virginia: The Enduring Dominion* (1988); J. Harvie Wilkinson's *Harry Byrd and the Changing Face of Virginia Politics* (1968); and Alden Hatch's *The Byrds of Virginia* (1969), which maps the dynasty back to William II for good measure. For the history of southern business development under Byrd's senate reign, the key text is Bruce J. Schulman's *From Cotton Belt to Sunbelt: Federal Policy, Economic Development, and the Transformation of the South 1938–1980* (1994), and I also learned much from Gavin Wright's "The New Deal and the Modernization of the South," from *Federal History 2010: 58–73.*

Byrd can be found lurking in Ira Katznelson's *Fear Itself: The New Deal and the Origins of Our Time* (2013) and even briefly in Studs Terkel's *Hard Times: An Oral History of the Great Depression* (1970). For the dark details of massive resistance and Prince Edward County's fight against school desegregation, one need only read Kristen Green's *Something Must Be Done About Prince Edward County* (2015).

For insights into Virginia's postwar mourning and memorial culture, the go-to is Drew Gilpin Faust's *This Republic of Suffering: Death and the American Civil War* (2008), though there is a particularly evocative firsthand account of this period in Richmond native James Branch Cabell's feisty, corrective Virginia ethnography, *Let Me Lie* (1947).

Chapter 4: A Museum and a Mountaintop

There is a short biographical essay on Julian Wood Glass Jr. on the Museum of the Shenandoah Valley's website, www.themsv. org. I learned additional details about his life and relationship from "Rearranging the Closet: Decoding the LGBT Exhibit Space," by Michael Lesperance in *InPark Magazine* #51 (2014), and "In Tribute to R. Lee Taylor," delivered by the Hon. Frank

R. Wolf of Virginia to the U.S. House of Representatives on Wednesday, June 28, 2000.

Chapter 5: How to Build a City

Berkeley Springs's reputation as an early-nineteenth-century spa destination can be gleaned from almost any book on Virginia in that era, though the specifics I used are taken from Jeanne Mozier and Betty Lou Harmison's Images of America volume on the town and from Jeanne's expertly curated work in the Museum of the Berkeley Springs. The twentieth-century descriptions of the town's post-glory sleepiness can be found in *The WPA Guide to West Virginia* (2014; originally published by the Federal Writer's Project as *West Virginia: A Guide to the Mountain State* [1941]) and *Shenandoah: The Valley Story* (1972) by Alvin Dohme, which is the "faded and broken-spined" book I quote at length.

For information on the growth of the bottled water industry, I relied on *Bottlemania* (2009) by Elizabeth Royte. My understanding of the state of water in West Virginia was aided by *"The Freedom Industries Spill: Lessons Learned and Needed Reforms"* (2014), a report written by the consulting group Downstream Strategies and the West Virginia Rivers Coalition.

Chapter 6: Toxically Pure

Joe Bageant published only one book in the United States, *Deer Hunting with Jesus* (2007), which, while essential, barely conveys his unbelievable prolificacy over the last eight or so years of his life. His current website, bageant.typepad.com, is still operated by Ken Smith, and will supply the curious reader with a seemingly infinite number of essays, responses to reader e-mails, diaries, and tossed-off ramblings. Better than any book, that website conveys the overwhelming productivity of Joe's mind during this final era, as well as his burdensome and obsessive personality.

His second book, *Rainbow Pie: A Redneck Memoir* (2010), is a wonderful portrait of mountain subsistence life and the values therein, and beautifully written. It was originally published in Australia and remains without a U.S. publisher as of this writing, though copies are easily obtained online or in Winchester-area bookstores.

Of his many, many other uncollected pieces, the one that provided the greatest insights for this chapter is a 2009 essay, "Skinny-Dipping in Reality: The Great Hippy LSD Enlightenment Search Party," which details his relationship with hallucinogens and the 1960s counterculture generally. It is also the essay that I think best exhibits Joe's worldview and talent for prose. It's stunning. "Skinny-Dipping in Reality" originally appeared on the website alternet.org.

For a great understanding of the back-to-the-land movement, I relied on Kate Daloz's *We Are As Gods* (2016) and *The 60s Communes: Hippies and Beyond* (1999) by Timothy Miller, though there is a huge and growing library surrounding the era, from academic work to memoirs.

For information on the growth of Virginia and Winchester's Hispanic population, I relied on U.S. Census Bureau figures and a few reports: "Immigrants, Politics, and Local Response in Suburban Washington" (2009) from the Brookings Institution, the Pew Research Center's "Demographic profile of Hispanics in Virginia, 2014," and "US Immigration: National and State Trends and Actions Overview" (2015) from the Pew Charitable Trusts.

A great number of friends and family submitted to be interviewed about Joe, which is a tribute to the effect he had on people at all stages of his life. These included his three children, Tim, Patrick, and Liz; his webmaster and fellow Mexican émigré Ken Smith; Ward Churchill and Jerry Roberts from the Boulder days; Scott Mason from the *Winchester Star;* Andy Gyurisin, onetime owner of the Winchester Book Gallery; Nick Smart, whose company I could see why Joe valued as he did; Rachel Klayman, the editor of *Deer Hunting with Jesus;* and obviously his widow, Barbara Dickinson, whose generosity and support were frankly shocking.

I must take the opportunity here to recommend Vine Deloria Jr.'s *Custer Died for Your Sins* (1969), which I contend was a major influence on *Deer Hunting with Jesus,* even down to the provocatively comic title. That's technically conjecture, however; I have yet to find any specific mention of that book among Joe's own writing, though he did dedicate a 2005 essay, "Carpooling with Adolf Eichmann" (again, provocatively comic), to Deloria and Ward Churchill.

Chapter 7: They'll Have to Carry Me Out

I know what I know about George Jones from Rich Kienzle's *The Grand Tour* (2016) and Nick Tosches's 1994 profile, also inevitably called "The Grand Tour," which is collected in *The Nick Tosches Reader* (2000).

Chapter 8: Better Neighbors

For information on the formation of Winchester's medical and health-care systems (and for many other insights into the region's development and expansion during the Byrd era), I relied on "Up to Date and Progressive: Winchester and Frederick County Virginia, 1870–1980" (2014), a dissertation by Mary Sullivan Linhart at George Mason University. Dr. Matt Hahn's *Distracted: How Regulations Are Destroying the Practice of Medicine and Preventing True Health-Care Reform* (2017) was an obvious source for his thoughts on administrative health-care obstacles, and for a welcome look at national health policy from the unlikely vantage point of Berkeley Springs and Hancock, Maryland. For coverage of Valley Health's various expansions and partnerships, I read innumerable articles in the *Winchester Star* and the *Washington Business Journal*. No surprise, there are additional comments (growls, really) about Valley Health and Winchester Medical Center in Joe Bageant's *Deer Hunting with Jesus* (2007).

For sources on the growth of Winchester-Frederick County's Hispanic population, see the notes on Chapter 6.

I relied on a number of articles and papers for general information on the state of modern rural health care and outcomes, including *"Rural Relevance 2017: Assessing the State of Rural Healthcare in America"* (2017), written by Michael Topchik for iVantage Health Analytics and the The Chartis Group; "Establishing and Maintaining Rural Public Health Infrastructure" (2012) by Michael Meit et al. for the NORC Walsh Center for Rural Health Analysis; and "How Has the ACA Changed Finances for Different Types of Hospitals? Updated Insights from

2015 Cost Report Data" (2017) by Fredric Blavin for the Robert Wood Johnson Foundation and the Urban Institute.

Chapter 9: Blessed to Be Gray

"On the wide level of a mountain's head" is the opening line of Samuel Taylor Coleridge's "Time, Real and Imaginary (An Allegory)," a poem that rumbled in my head for all the years I thought about Winchester and its inhabitants.